meatless
all day

meatless all day

Recipes for Inspired VEGETARIAN MEALS

Dina Cheney

Photography by Kate Sears

The Taunton Press

The Taunton Press
Inspiration for hands-on living®

The Taunton Press, Inc., 63 South Main Street
PO Box 5506, Newtown, CT 06470-5506
e-mail: tp@taunton.com

Editor: Carolyn Mandarano
Copy editor: Nina Rynd Whitnah
Indexer: Heidi Blough
Cover design: Rita Sowins / Sowins Design
Interior design and layout: Rita Sowins / Sowins Design
Art director: Rosalind Loeb Wanke
Photo editor: Erin Giunta
Photographer: Kate Sears/CarolMyersReps.com
Food stylist: Paul Grimes
Prop stylist: Angharad Bailey

Cover photographer: Kate Sears
Author photo: Richard Flaskegaard

The following names/manufacturers appearing in *Meatless All Day* are trademarks:
Bonne Maman®, Daiya™, Dufour®, Field Roast®, Geeta's®, Go Veggie!™, Lurpak®,
Maranatha®, Muir Glen®, Old Bay®, Organic Valley®, Sarabeth's®

Library of Congress Cataloging-in-Publication Data

Cheney, Dina, author.
   Meatless all day : recipes for inspired vegetarian meals / Dina Cheney.
      pages cm
   ISBN 978-1-62113-776-4 (paperback)
   1. Vegetarian cooking. I. Title.
   TX837.C4533 2014
   641.5'636--dc23

                              2013050950

Printed in the United States of America
10 9 8 7 6 5 4 3 2 1

To Koby

Acknowledgments

What a pleasure it's been to work on a second book with Carolyn Mandarano, my editor at The Taunton Press. I deeply appreciate her intelligence, kindness, consideration, and incredible competence. The sheer beauty of this book speaks for itself. For this, I thank the following in spades: art director Rosalind Wanke and photo editor Erin Giunta at Taunton, photographer Kate Sears, food stylist Paul Grimes, and prop stylist Angharad Bailey. Thanks also to the PR/marketing team: Missy Robinson, Janel Noblin, Erin Dubuque, and Audrey Locorotondo. My gratitude extends to the rest of the Taunton team, and to the following companies for sending me ingredients with which to develop recipes: Turtle Island Foods (tempeh), Vitasoy (tofu and fresh Asian noodles), and Thai Kitchen (Asian ingredients). Finally, thanks to my mother for recipe testing and to my family and friends, especially my husband, Koby. It is to him that I owe the gift of being able to pursue my passion.

contents

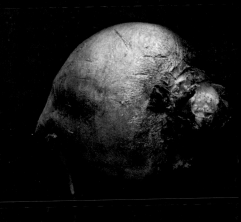

Mouthwatering Meatless Meals— Really!

VEGETARIAN, DELICIOUS, AND SUBSTANTIAL all in the same sentence? Yes, it can be done, and you only have to open this book to discover the possibilities. The secret is wielding savory, high-impact "power" ingredients. In the process of preparing the 85 colorful and flavorful entrées in this book, you will be convinced—whether your goal is to eat vegetarian for three meals a day, seven days a week, or just one meal one day.

Instead of the wan salads and bland tofu stir-fries typically associated with vegetarian fare, you'll find innovative spins on classics, such as beet Wellington (p. 176) and whole wheat spaghetti with white bean balls (p. 149), as well as ultimate versions of traditional dishes, like mac and cheese with manchego and *piquillo* peppers (p. 159).

The breakfast, lunch, and dinner entrées in these pages are so incredibly filling that some might even call them meaty. I dare you to prepare them for any avowed carnivores you know. I bet they won't miss the meat—especially since most dishes are full of protein, whether it comes from eggs, legumes, seeds, dairy products, or whole grains.

In addition to infusing dishes with the power ingredients found on pp. 8–9, read the cooking tips on the following pages to ensure that your meatless entrées come out perfectly. While the information here can be applied to all kinds of dishes—even those with meat!—it is particularly important when cooking vegetarian fare.

ᴄ⟨ Tips for Perfect Vegetables ⟩ᴐ

Naturally, vegetables hold an exalted position in a vegetarian cookbook, so it's key to prepare them properly to make them shine.

Before cooking vegetables or serving them raw, prep them to enhance their texture. For instance, remove the string from snow peas and the woody bottom few inches from asparagus. With vegetables whose parts have different densities, meaning they will cook at different rates (as with broccoli stalks and florets), separate them. Cut vegetables in pieces that are the same size so they finish cooking at the same time.

As a general rule, you should aim to retain vegetables' vibrant color and cook them just until crisp-tender (cooked through, but still with a slight bite). When vegetables lose their bright hue and develop a mushy or stringy texture, they've been overcooked. Still, you don't want to undercook them either—a common pitfall with hard types such as potatoes, carrots, and beets.

My favorite ways to cook vegetables are steaming, sautéing, stir-frying, and roasting briefly (after tossing in olive oil and salt and pepper) at 400° to 425°F. If boiling green vegetables, cook in lots of heavily salted water. To test for doneness, use a fork or sharp knife; if piercing through the vegetable requires a lot of effort, continue the cooking process. I usually taste as well—there are few more reliable ways to assess texture and flavor.

If you are not planning on serving green vegetables until later, blanch them in lots of heavily salted ice-cold water, swish for a couple of minutes, and drain. If you've just sautéed fresh spinach, drain on a clean towel prior to serving.

And, here's a tip about avocados, even though they're technically a fruit: cut them open at the last minute and drizzle with citrus juice to prevent browning.

ᴄ⟨ The Art of Cooking Eggs ⟩ᴐ

Eggs, with their rich and creamy texture (and high nutritional value), take center stage in many of these recipes. For this reason, using the freshest eggs you can find is paramount. Look for them at your local farm or farmers' market. You might pay a bit more than what you'd spend at the grocery store, but you'll be rewarded with beautiful yolks and exceptional flavor.

With scrambled eggs, you want to achieve a creamy and moist texture, with large, soft, blanket-like curds. To begin, first whisk together eggs with salt, pepper, and a small amount of milk or cream in a small bowl (I also love to add minced fresh chives). Then, melt butter over medium heat in a nonstick sauté pan. Once melted, add the eggs. Lower the heat to medium low and cook, using a small nonstick spatula to scrape the egg mixture from the perimeter to the center of the pan, letting the still-liquid eggs take its place. Repeat occasionally until the eggs are 90% cooked; then transfer immediately to a bowl or plate. (They will continue to cook a bit; don't let them overcook or they will become dry.)

When making hard-cooked eggs, add them to a heavy saucepan and then cover with 2 inches of cold water. Bring to a boil over high heat. Let the eggs boil for no more than 1 minute, and move the pan to a cold burner. Cover and let sit for 12 minutes (set the timer). Immediately pour the eggs into a colander set in the sink. Continuously run cold water over the eggs as you jostle them in the colander several times until the shells crack; peel the eggs under running water, too. Store hard-cooked eggs for up to a week in the fridge.

For fried eggs, melt butter in a nonstick sauté pan over medium heat. Once melted, crack one egg into a ramekin and then pour it gently into the hot butter; repeat with the other eggs, allotting some space between them. Sprinkle evenly with salt and pepper. Cook until the whites become opaque and are no longer runny and their edges turn slightly golden brown, about 3 minutes. Use a large spoon to baste the surface of the eggs with some of the melted butter. After another minute, cover the pan and reduce the heat to low. Cook until the yolks are done to your liking: either still bright yellow and slightly molten (maybe 30 seconds) or firmer (another minute or two). Immediately transfer to plates, and serve.

For poached eggs, add several inches of water (with a bit of salt and white vinegar) to a saucepan or deep frying pan. Heat over medium high until the water reaches a strong simmer, and then reduce to a gentle simmer over medium-low heat. Crack an egg into a ramekin and then gently pour into the lightly simmering water (repeat with more eggs). Poach until the whites are completely set and the yolks are cooked to your liking, 3 or 4 minutes. Use a spider or slotted spoon to transfer the poached egg(s) to a baking sheet lined with paper towels or a clean kitchen towel. Sprinkle with salt and pepper, and serve.

Tips for a Golden Brown, Crispy Exterior

One way to make food satisfying is to give it a golden brown, crispy-crunchy exterior. A golden brown exterior also looks appealing because the hue signals the presence of flavor, due to a chemical process called the Maillard reaction (if you're curious, it involves a heat-induced reaction between sugars and proteins that causes browning). Meanwhile, an exterior that shatters slightly when bitten into adds to the primal, sensual experience of eating.

When cooking in the sauté pan, dredge ingredients (such as tofu or eggplant slices or sweet potato cakes) in flour, and then sear in a small amount of fat over medium-high to high heat (the former if using a nonstick pan). Or, dredge in flour, coat in plain beaten egg or beaten egg mixed with mustard, and then coat in one or more of the following: breadcrumbs (traditional or crispier panko), crushed cornflakes, chopped nuts, even shredded unsweetened coconut. Next, pan-fry (in a few tablespoons of fat) in a shallow pan over medium to medium-high heat. Either way, don't crowd the pan; doing so makes food steam.

When a recipe calls for roasting, toss the ingredients with a bit of oil and spices and cook at a high heat (400–450°F) until tender, but not overly so. With some vegetables (such as potatoes), you're going for a golden brown color and slightly crisp texture. With others, such as asparagus, your goal is a vibrant green hue and just-tender texture.

MEATLESS ON MONDAY—AND BEYOND

The phrase "Meatless Monday" originated during World War I. President Herbert Hoover, who was head of the U. S. Food Administration, asked families to avoid eating meat on Mondays to help the war effort. To facilitate this, his office provided recipe booklets and menus. Impressively, more than 13 million families signed a pledge to participate. During World War II and beyond, Presidents Franklin D. Roosevelt and Harry S. Truman resurrected the movement. In 2003, so did former adman Sid Lerner (in association with the Johns Hopkins Bloomberg School of Public Health). The goal: to reduce meat consumption by 15% to improve public and environmental health. With increased vegetarianism and eco-consciousness, this nonprofit public health initiative has turned international. The Monday Campaigns—which runs the Meatless Monday program—has also expanded to encompass other health initiatives, such as cutting smoking and exercising. Visit www.meatlessmonday.com for information, toolkits, and recipes, all geared to help you decrease your meat intake.

Tips for Enhancing Meatiness

* **Drain tofu to help it brown and turn crisp before sautéing, pan-frying, stir-frying, or roasting.** Place a few layers of paper towels or clean kitchen towels on a large surface. Cover with pieces of tofu. Cover them with more layers of paper towels or clean towels, then top with a heavy plate or baking sheet. Let sit at room temperature for 20 to 30 minutes.

* **Caramelize onions to increase their sweetness and meatiness and reduce their volume.** Melt butter or heat oil in a sauté pan over medium heat. Once the butter has melted or the oil is hot, add thinly sliced onions and some salt, pepper, and—if desired—a pinch of brown sugar. Cook, stirring occasionally, until the onions are golden brown and very limp, about 30 minutes.

* **Toast nuts, seeds, shredded coconut, and bread to intensify and sweeten their flavor and to achieve a golden brown color and crispness.** With nuts, seeds, and shredded coconut, toast in the toaster oven on low or in a conventional oven at 350°F. Watch carefully, as they burn quickly; the process won't take more than 10 minutes. Cube bread, then toast in a conventional oven at 350° to 400°F until golden brown and crisp, 10 to 20 minutes.

* **Incorporate miso paste into liquids.** Miso paste can separate from liquids into which it is stirred. In a small bowl, whisk together the miso paste with a small amount of the liquid you'll be adding it to (such as hot soup stock). Then whisk the miso-liquid mixture into the pot with liquid. Do this right before serving.

* **Roast tomatoes to concentrate their flavor and remove excess water.** Halving plum tomatoes and then roasting them at a low heat (around 250°F) for 3 or 4 hours makes them taste sweeter—almost jam-like—and gives them a plump, voluptuous texture. After halving them, place them in one layer on a baking sheet with sides. Drizzle with olive oil and sprinkle with salt, pepper, chopped garlic, and fresh thyme.

* **Roast bell peppers to give them a smoky-sweet flavor and soft, velvety texture.** Place whole bell peppers directly on a gas burner or gas grill grates on high heat. Cook, turning with tongs, until blackened almost all over. (Alternatively, roast on a foil-lined baking sheet in a 450°F oven or under the broiler a few inches from the heat source and turn until all of the sides have blackened. The process should take 15 to 20 minutes if broiling or about a half hour if roasting.) Then, transfer to a plate, cover with a large, upside-down bowl, and let steam for about 15 minutes. Peel and discard the blackened skin; cut to remove and discard the stem and seeds; and slice the flesh.

* **Cook whole grains to achieve the optimum texture.** Add plenty of salt to the cooking water, follow directions on the package, and keep a close watch to prevent burning (sometimes, you might need to add more liquid).

* **Rehydrate dried fruit to soften it and, sometimes, add flavor.** Soak dried fruit in (sometimes hot) liquid, such as fruit juice, water, or alcohol for about 20 minutes.

Power Ingredients

I like to call the list of items here "power" ingredients, since they add a meaty flavor (dark, caramelized, savory, umami) or texture (satisfying, crunchy, rich, creamy, meat-like) to dishes. You'll find many of these ingredients in the recipes throughout the book. But don't be afraid to try the others listed here, either, especially if you want to amp up the flavor or texture in a dish.

FOR A MEATY FLAVOR

* Balsamic, black, and red-wine vinegars
* Barbecue sauce
* Black bean sauce
* Black tea
* Brown mustard
* Brown sweeteners, including maple syrup, brown sugar, honey, and molasses
* Caramelized onions
* Chiles and hot sauces (including Sriracha and chipotle en adobo)
* Cocktail sauce
* Cooked dark greens, such as spinach
* Curry paste
* Fig preserves
* Hoisin sauce
* Ketchup
* Liquid smoke
* Miso paste
* Nutritional yeast powder
* Nuts and nut products
* Pomegranate molasses
* Red wine, beer, and brown liquors (such as whisky)
* Roasted garlic
* Seaweed and seaweed seasoning mixtures
* Soy sauce
* Special salts, including smoked and sea (in particular, sel gris)
* Spices, including smoked paprika, black pepper, cinnamon, cumin, coriander, and nutmeg
* Tamarind paste

FOR A MEATY TEXTURE

* Avocados
* Bread cubes, especially pumpernickel
* Cauliflower
* Eggplant
* Plantains and bananas
* Potatoes (including sweet)
* Squash, including zucchini and pumpkin

- Beans, peas, lentils
- Beets
- Capers and olives
- Carrots
- Dairy products (including cheeses such as smoked mozzarella, Parmigiano-Reggiano, pecorino, Manchego, and feta; brown butter; and yogurt)
- Dried fruit, especially prunes, apricots, and raisins
- Eggs
- Fresh and dried mushrooms
- Milks: cow, coconut, soy, nut, rice, flax, and more
- Roasted bell and chile peppers
- Tofu, tempeh, edamame, and seitan
- Tomatoes in all of their forms: fresh, canned, paste, roasted, sun-dried
- Whole grains

UMAMI-RICH INGREDIENTS

Many of my power ingredients, including those below, are umami-rich, or high in the fifth (savory) taste. (The other four tastes are sweet, salty, bitter, and sour or tart.) In science jargon, according to the Umami Information Center, this means that they include glutamate, a type of amino acid, and ribonucleotides, including inosinate and guanylate.

- Carrots
- Chinese cabbage
- Eggs
- Green tea
- Mushrooms
- Parmesan cheese
- Potatoes
- Seaweed
- Soybeans
- Sweet potatoes
- Tomatoes

breakfast
& brunch

WAKE UP TO SOME FRESH APPROACHES TO THE MORNING MEAL. Here, PB&J is interpreted as French toast, while risotto gains unexpected sweetness from fresh strawberries and strawberry preserves. Meanwhile, pancakes take a savory turn—try the corn flapjacks with black bean salsa and Cheddar. Instead of always serving hotcakes with maple syrup, try my four fruit accompaniments—one for each season. What do you get when you cross Mideastern and American pastries? Baklava sticky buns, enlivened with the crunch of pistachios and sweetened with orange juice–laced syrup. And forget plain old scrambled eggs. Here, eggs are poached in tomato sauce and served with garlic toasts; or fried and topped with avocado and poblano salsa; or baked with toasted bread, sundried tomatoes, and mushrooms into a savory bread pudding. The list goes on, deliciously.

Strata with Cremini Mushrooms, Olives, and Sun-Dried Tomatoes

SERVES 8 TO 10

This savory bread pudding—full of Provençal flavors—is ideal for brunch, lunch, or dinner. If you want to make the strata ahead, complete every step prior to baking. Then immediately cover it and refrigerate. Bake the strata the next day, right before you're ready to serve. Make sure to use a flavorful bread (the loaf I prefer contains rye flour and wheat bran), and purchase it unsliced, so you can cube it yourself.

1 large loaf country bread, such as *pain de campagne* (8 cups 1-inch cubes)

2 tablespoons extra-virgin olive oil, divided

2 tablespoons minced garlic

1¼ pounds cremini mushrooms, stems removed and caps sliced ¼ inch thick

1½ teaspoons coarse salt, divided

11 grinds fresh black pepper, divided

4 sprigs fresh thyme

One 8.3-ounce jar sun-dried tomatoes packed in oil

30 pitted jarred Kalamata olives, coarsely chopped

5 large eggs

2½ cups whole milk

1 cup half-and-half

3 tablespoons minced fresh chives

2 tablespoons Dijon mustard

1 tablespoon lemon zest

1. Heat the oven to 400°F. Place the bread cubes in one layer on a baking sheet with sides. Toast until lightly golden brown and slightly dried out, about 15 minutes. Carefully pour the bread into a large bowl and let it cool to room temperature. Reduce the oven temperature to 350°F.

2. Heat 1 tablespoon of the oil in a 12-inch, heavy, nonstick sauté pan over medium-high heat. When hot but not smoking, add the garlic, and sauté until aromatic, no more than 1 minute (you don't want it to burn). Immediately add the mushrooms plus ½ teaspoon salt, 5 grinds pepper, and the fresh thyme. Sauté until the mushrooms are tender and the majority of liquid has evaporated, 10 to 11 minutes. Set the mushrooms off the heat to cool, and pick out and discard the thyme sprigs.

3. Pour the sun-dried tomatoes into a colander set in the sink to drain. Rinse with water, and drain again. Squeeze the tomatoes to further drain, then coarsely chop (you should have about 1 heaping packed cup). Add the tomatoes and olives to the bread cubes in the bowl and mix well.

4. Crack the eggs into a medium bowl, and whisk well until smooth. Add the milk, half-and-half, chives, mustard, lemon zest, red pepper flakes, the remaining 1 teaspoon salt, and the remaining 6 grinds pepper. Whisk well to blend into a homogenous, cream-colored custard (no yellow egg yolk should be visible).

¼ teaspoon crushed red pepper flakes

2 cups freshly grated Gruyère, divided

8 ounces fresh goat cheese, crumbled, divided

5. Grease a 9 x 13 x 2-inch (3-quart) baking dish with the remaining 1 tablespoon of oil, and place it on a baking sheet with sides (the latter will catch any potential spills). Pour half of the bread-tomato-olive mixture into the baking dish in one even layer, then sprinkle with half of the Gruyère and goat cheese in one even layer. Ladle half of the custard mixture on top to coat well. Sprinkle the remaining bread-tomato-olive mixture in one even layer, then add the remaining Gruyère and goat cheese in an even layer. Ladle the remaining custard on top to coat well, using your hands to push the solids down to saturate them.

6. Bake the strata until the center is firm and the bread puffs up a bit and turns a light golden brown color, about 1 hour. Let cool slightly and serve.

SERVING SUGGESTIONS: This strata pairs beautifully with fruit. For breakfast or brunch, slice up some ripe melons, peaches, and apricots. If eating the strata for lunch or dinner, pair it with an herb salad, and cap the meal with an apricot and almond tart.

Broccoli, Smoked Mozzarella, and Roasted Red Pepper Frittata

Smoked mozzarella (which has a savory, meaty quality), salty Parmigiano-Reggiano, sweet roasted red peppers, and broccoli (with its vegetal and slightly bitter flavor) add up to a complex, balanced, and satisfying breakfast or brunch dish. Save the broccoli stalks for soup or salad.

10 large eggs

¾ teaspoon coarse salt, divided

16 grinds black pepper, divided

⅛ teaspoon crushed red pepper flakes

3 tablespoons extra-virgin olive oil, divided

1½ teaspoons finely chopped garlic

3 cups 1½-inch broccoli florets

One 12-ounce jar roasted red peppers, drained well and coarsely chopped

½ pound smoked mozzarella, thinly sliced

½ heaping packed cup freshly grated Parmigiano-Reggiano

1. Heat the oven to 375°F. In a large bowl, whisk together the eggs, ½ teaspoon salt, 8 grinds pepper, and the red pepper flakes until smooth. Set aside. Heat 2 tablespoons oil in a heavy, nonstick, oven-proof frying pan over medium heat.

2. When the oil is hot, add the garlic and sauté until aromatic, about 1 minute. Immediately add the remaining oil and the broccoli (you don't want the garlic to burn). Sprinkle the broccoli evenly with ¼ teaspoon salt and 8 grinds pepper, and sauté until tender but still slightly firm, about 5 minutes (poke with a fork to check).

3. Make sure the broccoli florets are evenly spaced in one layer, and then pour in the seasoned egg mixture. Gently shake the pan so the eggs spread evenly. Arrange the peppers and cheeses evenly over the top of the frittata, and let it continue to cook until the edges are set, about another 4 minutes.

4. Transfer to the oven, and cook until the eggs are firm and the cheese has melted, about 15 minutes. Let cool slightly, then serve straight from the pan or on a platter pepper side up.

SERVING SUGGESTIONS: Serve the frittata alongside arugula tossed with lemon vinaigrette and wedges of ciabatta. For dessert, set out berries with zabaglione.

Open-Face Fried Egg Sandwiches with Avocado and Poblano Salsa

Prepare the avocado mixture and toast the bread right before serving. If you don't like cilantro, go with fresh parsley instead. Cook the yolks to your preferred degree of doneness; if anyone with a compromised immune system (pregnant, elderly, ill, or very young) is dining at your table, cook them all the way through, until no longer molten.

FOR THE SALSA

- **1 poblano pepper**
- **⅓ cup finely chopped red onions**
- **1 cup canned no-salt-added, fire-roasted diced tomatoes, drained**
- **⅓ cup finely chopped fresh cilantro leaves**
- **1 tablespoon fresh-squeezed, strained lime juice**
- **½ teaspoon coarse salt**

FOR THE AVOCADO SPREAD

- **1 cup mashed avocado flesh**
- **1 tablespoon fresh-squeezed, strained lime juice**
- **¼ teaspoon coarse salt**
- **5 grinds black pepper**

MAKE THE SALSA

Place the poblano directly on a gas burner and heat on high. Roast, turning with tongs, until each side is completely blackened, about 8 minutes total (alternatively, roast in the oven until blackened). Place an overturned bowl on top of the pepper and steam until the blackened portion is easy to remove, about 20 minutes. Peel off the charred skin, remove the stem and seeds, and chop the flesh into small dice. Set aside ⅓ cup of this diced pepper. Meanwhile, place the red onions in a small bowl and cover with cold water. Soak for 20 minutes and then drain. Place the diced roasted pepper, drained red onions, diced tomatoes, cilantro, lime juice, and salt in a medium bowl; mix well.

MAKE THE AVOCADO SPREAD

In a small bowl, stir together all of the ingredients. Set aside.

COOK THE EGGS AND MAKE THE SANDWICHES

1. Heat 2 tablespoons of the butter over medium heat in each of two 10-inch, heavy, nonstick sauté pans. Once it's melted, crack 4 eggs into 4 ramekins (1 egg in each ramekin). Carefully pour the 4 eggs into one of the pans, trying not to overlap them. Repeat by cracking the remaining 4 eggs into 4 ramekins and then pouring them into the other pan.

FOR THE EGGS AND SANDWICHES

4 tablespoons (½ stick) unsalted butter

8 large eggs

¼ teaspoon coarse salt

Four 1-inch-thick slices good-quality country or challah bread, toasted

2. Cook the eggs for 4 minutes, basting them a bit with the melted butter, and then reduce the heat to low and cover (ideally with a large glass pan lid) until the whites are a bit golden brown around the edges and the yolks are still just very slightly molten, about 2 minutes (the butter might splatter a bit). For diners who prefer their yolks fully cooked, cook the eggs slightly longer. Evenly sprinkle with the salt.

3. Place a bread slice on each of four plates. Top each one with some avocado spread, 2 eggs, and some salsa. Serve immediately.

SERVING SUGGESTION: Serve these Mexican-inspired sandwiches with fresh guava juice, coffee, and tropical fruit parfaits for a rousing, gorgeous breakfast.

Eggs Poached in Tomato Sauce with Garlicky Grilled Bread

SERVES 4

Based on a traditional Italian dish, this entrée consists of lightly poached eggs in homemade tomato sauce. The eggs are sprinkled with fresh parsley and served with crisp, garlicky country bread. Feel free to double the quantity of bread, if you'd like to serve two slices with each portion.

¼ cup plus 2 tablespoons extra-virgin olive oil, divided

2 tablespoons plus 2 teaspoons minced garlic, divided

⅛ teaspoon crushed red pepper flakes

Two 28-ounce cans strained unsalted tomatoes, such as Muir Glen®

6 sprigs fresh oregano, tied together with kitchen twine

1¼ teaspoons coarse salt, divided

13 grinds black pepper, divided

8 large eggs

¼ cup finely chopped fresh flat-leaf parsley leaves

Four ¼-inch-thick slices country bread

¼ teaspoon sea salt, such as sel gris

1. Heat the oven to 375°F. In a small bowl, mix together 3 tablespoons of the oil with the 2 teaspoons of minced garlic. Let sit for 15 minutes (or more), and then pour the oil into a small strainer set over a small bowl, reserving the flavored oil and discarding the garlic. Set the garlic oil aside.

2. While the garlic steeps in the oil, heat 1 tablespoon oil in a medium-sized, heavy saucepan with high sides over medium heat. When hot, add the remaining 2 tablespoons garlic and the red pepper flakes and sauté until aromatic, no more than 1 minute. Immediately add the tomatoes, oregano, 1 teaspoon salt, and 5 grinds pepper; raise the heat to medium high and simmer until thick and reduced by about a third, about 30 minutes (you should yield about 4 cups of sauce). Carefully remove and discard the oregano. Let the sauce sit off the heat until it reaches room temperature.

3. Pour the sauce into a 9 x 13 x 2-inch glass casserole dish. One at a time, crack an egg into a ramekin, and then gently pour it on top of the sauce. Repeat with the remaining eggs, trying not to overlap them (you should end up with eight evenly spaced yolks in the dish). Sprinkle the eggs evenly with a total of ¼ teaspoon salt and 8 grinds pepper. Bake the eggs until the whites are completely set and the yolks are almost set but still slightly runny, 18 to 21 minutes. Remove from the oven, and sprinkle evenly with the parsley.

4. Right when the eggs go into the oven, brush both sides of the bread slices with the reserved garlic oil (use all of it). Brush a medium-sized, heavy, nonstick grill pan with the remaining 1 tablespoon oil, and heat over medium high. When hot, add the bread and toast until golden, crisp, and slightly charred on each side, turning over halfway through, about 15 minutes total. Sprinkle the bread slices evenly with the sea salt.

5. Using a large spatula without holes, divide the eggs-in-sauce among four plates; serve a slice of grilled bread alongside.

SERVING SUGGESTION: These eggs are delicious with a citrus salad (grapefruit and orange slices with shaved fennel).

TRY THIS: Did you know that you can poach eggs ahead of time? Just cook and store in water. Reheat in gently simmering water for about a minute, then drain.

Scrambled Eggs with Chives and Mushroom-Maple Bundles

SERVES 4

Here's a vegetarian version of scrambled eggs with sausage. Taking some inspiration from the United Kingdom (where roasted mushrooms are often served with eggs for breakfast), I came up with these stuffed mushrooms that mimic the flavor of pork sausage. The rich, buttery mushrooms, with maple syrup and sage, will satisfy any sausage-lover. Begin melting the butter to cook the eggs when the mushrooms have been in the oven for about 10 minutes, and serve with jam-slathered toast.

FOR THE MUSHROOM-MAPLE BUNDLES

10 ounces white button mushrooms

4 tablespoons (½ stick) unsalted butter, 2 tablespoons melted, divided

¼ plus ⅛ teaspoon coarse salt, divided

¼ cup finely chopped red onions

1 tablespoon finely chopped garlic

2 teaspoons minced fresh sage leaves

¼ cup whole wheat panko breadcrumbs

5 grinds black pepper

Pinch crushed red pepper flakes

1 tablespoon maple syrup

continued

MAKE THE BUNDLES

1. Heat the oven to 400°F. Grease a baking sheet with cooking spray. Remove the stems from the mushrooms and discard. Turn the mushrooms so their undersides are facing up. Use a melon baller to gently and carefully scoop out their centers. Finely chop these centers, and set aside (you should yield about 3 tablespoons).

2. Place the mushroom caps, undersides facing up, close together on the baking sheet. Drizzle evenly with the 2 tablespoons melted butter and sprinkle evenly with the ⅛ teaspoon salt. Spread the mushrooms apart.

3. Melt the remaining 2 tablespoons butter in a 10-inch nonstick sauté pan over medium-high heat. When melted, add the chopped mushroom centers, onions, garlic, and sage, and sauté until the onions are softened and the mixture is aromatic, about 4 minutes. Add the breadcrumbs, the remaining ¼ teaspoon salt, the black pepper, and the red pepper flakes, and sauté until the breadcrumbs look crisp and golden, about another 3 minutes. Remove from the heat and stir in the maple syrup; mix well to distribute the syrup throughout.

continued

FOR THE SCRAMBLED EGGS

8 large eggs

¼ cup plus 2 tablespoons
   minced fresh chives

3 tablespoons 2% milk

½ teaspoon coarse salt

8 grinds black pepper

2 tablespoons unsalted butter

4. With the melon baller (or your fingers), spoon the stuffing into the mushroom cavities, packing it in. Bake until the mushrooms are tender and the stuffing is golden brown, about 20 minutes (watch carefully, as you don't want the sweet stuffing to burn).

COOK THE EGGS

1. While the mushrooms are baking, cook the eggs. In a medium bowl, whisk together the first five ingredients. Melt the butter in a nonstick 10-inch sauté pan over medium heat. Once the butter has melted, reduce the heat to medium low and pour in the eggs.

2. After a couple of minutes, use a rubber spatula to begin gently pushing the egg mixture from the edges to the center of the pan. Wait another minute or so, then repeat the process, continuing to gently scrape the eggs away from the sides of the pan (don't let the eggs form a skin around the sides of the pan and don't let the bottom of the eggs turn brown). You're going for silky, tender, yellow eggs—imagine a loosely ruffled yellow blanket. As soon as the eggs look barely wet (after they've been in the pan for about 5 minutes), immediately remove them from the heat.

3. Serve the hot eggs and mushrooms immediately.

TRY THIS: Make this dish vegan by substituting trans-fat-free margarine or olive oil for the butter in the mushrooms. Instead of eggs, whip up a tofu scramble.

Oven-Roasted Tomato, Zucchini, and Goat Cheese Frittata

SERVES 4 TO 6

Roasting the tomatoes concentrates their flavor and also makes them less juicy, so they don't water down the frittata. Roast them a day ahead; store, tightly covered, in the fridge until ready to use.

FOR THE OVEN-ROASTED TOMATOES

8 plum tomatoes, halved vertically

¼ cup extra-virgin olive oil

3 tablespoons fresh thyme leaves

2 teaspoons finely chopped garlic

¾ teaspoon coarse salt

16 grinds black pepper

FOR THE FRITTATA

10 large eggs

⅓ cup minced fresh chives

1 heaping teaspoon lemon zest

¾ teaspoon coarse salt, divided

13 grinds black pepper, divided

3 tablespoons extra-virgin olive oil, divided

1 tablespoon finely chopped garlic

1 small zucchini, trimmed and sliced thinly on the bias

4 ounces fresh goat cheese

1. Make the roasted tomatoes: Heat the oven to 250°F. Line a baking sheet with aluminum foil. Place the tomatoes, cut side up, on the foil. Drizzle with the oil and sprinkle evenly with the thyme, garlic, salt, and pepper. Roast until soft and semi-dried out, about 4 hours.

2. When ready to make the frittata, heat the oven to 375°F. In a medium bowl, whisk together the eggs, chives, lemon zest, ½ teaspoon salt, and 8 grinds pepper until smooth. Set aside.

3. Heat 2 tablespoons of the oil in a medium-sized, heavy non-stick, ovenproof frying pan over medium heat. When it's hot, add the garlic and sauté until aromatic, about 1 minute (don't let it burn). Immediately add the remaining 1 tablespoon oil and the zucchini. Sprinkle the zucchini evenly with ¼ teaspoon salt and 5 grinds pepper, and sauté until tender but still slightly firm, about 3 minutes (poke with a fork to check).

4. Make sure the zucchini are evenly spaced in one layer, and then pour in the seasoned egg mixture. Gently shake the pan so the eggs spread evenly. Arrange the tomatoes and cheese evenly over the top of the eggs, and let them cook until the edges are set, 4 to 5 minutes.

5. Transfer to the oven and cook until the eggs are firm and the cheese has melted, 15 minutes. Let cool slightly, then serve from the pan or transfer to a platter tomato side up and serve.

SERVING SUGGESTIONS: This frittata is a meal in itself for breakfast, but mixed fresh fruit is a nice accompaniment. If serving for lunch or dinner, pair with a baguette and green salad tossed with mustard vinaigrette; for dessert, try fresh plums or a plum clafouti.

Sweet and Savory Corn Pancakes with Black Bean Salsa

SERVES 4 TO 6; MAKES ABOUT 27 PANCAKES

Crisp and puffy on the outside and tender and moist within, these sweet corn-studded flapjacks are a full meal—especially when paired with the black bean salsa (feel free to double the salsa recipe if you want hefty portions). ¶ Sometimes, I like to give these pancakes a sweeter spin, and serve them with sour cream plus ancho maple syrup. To make the syrup, heat ½ cup maple syrup and ¼ teaspoon ancho chili powder in a small heavy saucepan over medium heat until simmering. Turn off the heat and let the syrup sit for a few minutes. ¶ If you like, heat the oven to 250°F to keep already-cooked pancakes warm while you cook the remaining batter.

FOR THE PANCAKES

2 cups frozen corn kernels, thawed

1½ cups grated mild Cheddar

1½ cups corn flour or finely ground cornmeal

1½ cups unbleached all-purpose flour

3 tablespoons granulated sugar

2 teaspoons baking soda

1½ teaspoons coarse salt

½ teaspoon ground cumin

¼ teaspoon ancho chili powder

2 cups buttermilk

3 large eggs, beaten

3 tablespoons unsalted butter, melted

Scant ½ cup vegetable oil, for cooking the pancakes

MAKE THE PANCAKES

1. In a large bowl, whisk together the first nine ingredients until well combined. In a medium bowl, whisk together the buttermilk, beaten eggs, and melted butter. Pour the liquid mixture into the dry mixture, and using a wooden spoon, gently mix well, just until combined.

2. Heat 2 tablespoons of the oil in a heavy 12-inch nonstick sauté pan over medium heat. When hot, use a ¼-cup measure to pour 5 pancakes into the pan. When they puff up and form lots of tiny holes (after about 3 minutes), carefully flip them over and cook the other side until the center is cooked through, about another 3 minutes.

3. Add 1 tablespoon of oil and repeat with another 5 pancakes. Continue cooking the pancakes, adding about 1 tablespoon of oil before each batch, until all of the pancakes are cooked.

FOR THE BLACK BEAN SALSA

One 15-ounce can black beans, rinsed and drained

⅓ cup finely chopped red bell peppers

⅓ cup finely chopped red onions

2 tablespoons fresh-squeezed, strained orange juice

1 tablespoon fresh-squeezed, strained lime juice

1 tablespoon liquid from canned chipotles en adobo

½ teaspoon coarse salt

¼ teaspoon ground cumin

FOR SERVING

Diced avocado

Sour cream

Chopped fresh cilantro leaves

MAKE THE SALSA

Gently mix together the salsa ingredients in a medium bowl. Do this right before serving the pancakes, so the salsa looks most attractive.

TO SERVE

Serve the pancakes warm, with some black bean salsa, avocado, sour cream, and cilantro.

SERVING SUGGESTION: To gild the lily, you can add fried eggs and vegetarian bacon.

TRY THIS: These pancakes are also delicious with Monterey Jack or pepper jack cheese. Serve with different salsas, too: peach, mango, tomatillo, or tomato-based.

Ricotta Pancakes with Berry Sauce

Lightly scented with lemon, these tender pancakes pair perfectly with the warm, sweet berry sauce. Serve alone or with vegetarian bacon.

FOR THE BERRY SAUCE

4 cups frozen mixed berries

¾ cup granulated sugar

¼ cup fresh-squeezed, strained lemon juice

¼ teaspoon coarse salt

½ teaspoon vanilla bean paste or pure vanilla extract

FOR THE PANCAKES

3 large eggs, divided

2 cups 2% milk

1½ cups part-skim ricotta

1 tablespoon lemon zest

2½ cups unbleached all-purpose flour

¼ cup granulated sugar

1½ teaspoons coarse salt

1 teaspoon baking powder

About ½ cup vegetable oil, for cooking the pancakes

MAKE THE SAUCE

Place all of the sauce ingredients, except the vanilla, in a medium-sized, heavy saucepot, and bring to a boil over medium-high heat. Simmer until a relatively thick liquid forms, stirring occasionally, 20 to 25 minutes. Stir in the vanilla and keep warm.

MAKE THE PANCAKES

1. With a hand mixer (or in a standing mixer), whip the egg whites on medium speed until they form soft peaks, 6 to 7 minutes. Set aside.

2. In a medium bowl, whisk together the egg yolks, milk, ricotta, and lemon zest until well blended. In a large bowl, whisk together the flour, sugar, salt, and baking powder.

3. With a wooden spoon, stir the yolk-milk mixture into the dry ingredients and mix just until combined (don't overmix). With a rubber spatula, gently fold in the egg whites, being careful not to overmix (you don't want to deflate the eggs).

4. Heat 2 tablespoons of the oil in a 12-inch, heavy, nonstick sauté pan over medium heat. When hot, use a ¼-cup measure to pour 5 pancakes into the pan. When they puff up and form lots of tiny holes (after about 2 minutes), carefully flip them over and cook the other side until the center is cooked through, about another 2 minutes.

5. Add 1 tablespoon of oil and repeat with another 5 pancakes. Continue cooking the pancakes, adding about 1 tablespoon of oil to the pan before each batch, until all of the pancakes are cooked. Serve immediately, drizzled with the berry sauce or with the sauce on the side.

Four-Season Buttermilk Pancakes

Within a half hour, these light, tender pancakes can be on the table—all year long. Pair them with one of these four sauces to give them a different look—and taste—each time the season changes. By the way, this batter also makes delicate, crisp waffles.

2 cups unbleached all-purpose flour

2 tablespoons granulated sugar

1 teaspoon baking powder

1 teaspoon baking soda

½ teaspoon coarse salt

1¾ cups buttermilk, well-shaken

¼ cup 2% milk

4 tablespoons (½ stick) unsalted butter, melted

2 large eggs

2 teaspoons pure vanilla extract

About ¼ cup vegetable oil

One of the seasonal sauces, for serving (recipes follow)

1. In a medium-sized bowl, whisk together the first 5 ingredients until well combined. Pour the buttermilk and milk into a large graduated liquid measuring cup. Add the melted butter, eggs, and vanilla, and mix very well. Pour the liquid ingredients into the center of the dry ingredients. Stir until thoroughly mixed, but still a bit lumpy (do not overmix).

2. Brush 1 tablespoon of oil over the entire interior of a 10-inch, heavy, nonstick frying pan, and heat over medium. When the oil is hot, use a ¼-cup measure to pour 4 pancakes into the pan. Cook until the first side is golden brown, about 2 minutes. Carefully flip and cook the other side until also golden brown, about another 2 minutes. Keep the pancakes warm in a 250°F oven. Repeat with the remaining batter, adding about 1 tablespoon oil to the pan with each batch. Serve immediately with one of the seasonal sauces.

WINTER GINGERED CITRUS WITH HONEY

MAKES ABOUT 2 CUPS

3 navel oranges

2 tablespoons honey or granulated sugar

1¼ teaspoons minced crystallized ginger

1 teaspoon lime zest

⅛ teaspoon coarse salt

1. Using a sharp chef's knife, cut the peel and tops and bottoms off the oranges. Cut between the segments to release them, removing the membranes. Place the orange segments in a medium bowl (you should have 2 cups).

2. Squeeze the peel and membranes left over from segmenting the oranges into a bowl. Pour ¼ cup of this orange juice into a small bowl, then add the remaining ingredients. Mix well and pour over the orange segments. Mix gently. Serve the citrus wedges alongside the pancakes, spooning some of the liquid over the hotcakes in lieu of syrup.

SPRINGTIME STRAWBERRY-RHUBARB SAUCE

MAKES 1 CUP

2 cups hulled and quartered
   fresh strawberries

1 cup thinly sliced trimmed
   fresh rhubarb

¼ cup plus 2 tablespoons
   granulated sugar

2 tablespoons fresh-squeezed,
   strained lemon juice

⅛ teaspoon coarse salt

Place all the ingredients in a medium-sized, heavy saucepan over medium-high heat. Cook, stirring occasionally, until the sauce becomes smooth and reduces to 1 cup, about 15 minutes. Serve warm or at room temperature.

SUMMER BLUEBERRY MAPLE SYRUP

MAKES 1¼ TO 1½ CUPS

2 cups fresh or frozen
   blueberries

1 cup maple syrup

Place the ingredients in a medium-sized, heavy saucepan and heat over medium-high heat. Cook, stirring occasionally, until the sauce thickens and reduces to 1½ to 1¼ cups, about 19 minutes. Serve warm.

FALL PEARS SAUTÉED WITH MAPLE SYRUP

MAKES ABOUT 2½ CUPS

2 tablespoons unsalted butter

2 Anjou or Bartlett pears,
   halved, cored, and sliced
   ⅓ inch thick

⅓ cup maple syrup

¼ teaspoon coarse salt

⅛ teaspoon ground cinnamon

⅛ teaspoon ground cardamom

Heat the butter in a 10-inch heavy sauté pan over medium heat. Once melted, add the pears in one layer and sauté for 2 minutes. Add the remaining ingredients and sauté, stirring gently and occasionally, until the pears are tender and coated with the sauce and the sauce has thickened just slightly, another 3 to 4 minutes. Serve warm.

SERVING SUGGESTION: To complete the meal, add some scrambled eggs, coffee, and juice.

Pumpkin Pear Pancakes

These rich pancakes—ideal for fall entertaining—have the tender, cakey texture of the crêpe-like French dessert clafouti. The combination of spices gives them a warm, complex, pumpkin pie-like flavor. Be sure to use ripe, sweet pears, and slice them at the last minute to avoid browning.

3 large eggs, divided

2 cups 2% milk

1½ cups canned pumpkin purée

2 tablespoons melted unsalted butter

1 teaspoon pure vanilla extract

3 cups unbleached all-purpose flour

¼ cup plus 1 tablespoon light brown sugar

1½ teaspoons coarse salt

1¼ teaspoons baking powder

½ teaspoon ground cinnamon

¼ teaspoon ground ginger

¼ teaspoon ground allspice

¼ teaspoon ground nutmeg

¼ teaspoon ground cloves

About ¼ cup vegetable oil, for cooking the pancakes

3 ripe Anjou or Bartlett pears, halved, cored, and sliced ¼ inch thick

1. With a hand mixer (or in a standing mixer), whip the egg whites on medium speed until they form soft peaks, 6 to 7 minutes. Set aside.

2. In a medium bowl, whisk together the egg yolks, milk, pumpkin, melted butter, and vanilla until well blended. In a large bowl, whisk together the flour, sugar, salt, baking powder, cinnamon, ginger, allspice, nutmeg, and cloves.

3. With a wooden spoon, stir the yolk-milk mixture into the dry ingredients and mix just until combined (don't overmix). With a rubber spatula, gently fold in the egg whites in three additions, being careful not to overmix (you don't want to deflate the eggs).

4. Heat 1 tablespoon of oil in a 10-inch, heavy, nonstick sauté pan or nonstick griddle over medium heat. When hot, use a ¼-cup measure to pour 4 pancakes into the pan. Place 2 pear slices on top of each pancake. When the pancakes puff up and form lots of tiny holes (after about 2 to 3 minutes), carefully flip them over and cook the other side until the center is cooked through, about another 2 minutes. Keep warm in a 250°F oven. Continue cooking the pancakes in batches, keeping the pan greased by adding about another 3 tablespoons of oil total in the process. Serve immediately.

SERVING SUGGESTION: Serve solo (trust me, they are plenty sweet and flavorful on their own) or with homemade or store-bought whole-berry cranberry sauce.

Date-Nut-Rum Bread

SERVES 4; MAKES ONE 8½ X 4¼ X 3-INCH LOAF

Cocoa powder, dark rum, and dark brown sugar add richness to this moist, dense quick bread, which makes a delicious tea sandwich, breakfast, snack, or dessert.

2 cups coarsely chopped pitted Medjool dates

¼ cup dark rum

2 cups plus 1 tablespoon unbleached all-purpose flour, divided

¼ cup unsweetened cocoa powder

2½ teaspoons minced crystallized ginger

1½ teaspoons baking powder

1 teaspoon ground cinnamon

1 teaspoon kosher salt

½ teaspoon baking soda

5 tablespoons (½ stick plus 1 tablespoon) unsalted butter, at room temperature

¾ cup maple syrup

2 tablespoons packed dark brown sugar

2 large eggs

2 teaspoons pure vanilla extract

1 cup coarsely chopped walnuts

1. Heat the oven to 350°F. Soak the dates in the rum for about 20 minutes. Spray an 8½ x 3-inch loaf pan with cooking spray.

2. In a medium-sized bowl, use a whisk to thoroughly mix 2 cups of flour, the cocoa powder, crystallized ginger, baking powder, cinnamon, salt, and baking soda.

3. In a large bowl and using an electric mixer, beat the butter with the maple syrup and brown sugar on medium speed until well-combined, about 3 minutes. Add the eggs and vanilla; beat until well-combined, about 1 minute. Reduce the mixer speed to low and add the flour mixture, beating until just combined, about 30 seconds (do not overmix).

4. In a small bowl, mix the walnuts with the remaining 1 table-spoon flour. Drain the dates, discarding the rum (or save it for another use). With a wooden spoon, gently stir the dates and walnuts into the batter. Pour the batter into the prepared pan and use a rubber spatula to even out the top.

5. Bake on the center rack of the oven until a toothpick inserted in the center of the bread comes out with some moist crumbs (but not wet batter), 45 to 50 minutes (do not overbake). Let cool in the pan for 10 minutes and then remove from the pan and transfer to a wire rack to finish cooling.

SERVING SUGGESTIONS: If serving this bread for breakfast, accompany it with fresh berries and plenty of coffee. For a lunch or brunch tea sandwich, spread with cream cheese, top with sliced strawberries, and serve open faced. Slather with lemon curd if serving for an afternoon snack or dessert.

Potato and Cheddar Latkes with Brown Sugar Applesauce

SERVES 4; MAKES ABOUT 20 LATKES AND 2 CUPS APPLESAUCE

Molten Cheddar oozes out of the centers of these crisp-on-the-outside, tender-on-the-inside latkes, making them more substantial. Don't skip the step of squeezing out excess liquid from the potatoes (opt for Idaho or Russet) and onions; it helps make the latkes crisp.

FOR THE APPLESAUCE

5½ cups coarsely chopped peeled, tart apples, such as Granny Smith

¼ cup plus 2 tablespoons apple cider

¼ cup light brown sugar

3 tablespoons fresh-squeezed, strained lemon juice

¼ plus ⅛ teaspoon coarse salt

FOR THE LATKES

2 pounds peeled baking potatoes such as Idaho or Russet, grated

1 cup finely chopped white onions

2 cups grated mild Cheddar

¼ cup unbleached all-purpose flour or matzoh meal

2 large eggs, beaten

1½ teaspoons coarse salt

8 grinds black pepper

About ¼ cup plus 1 tablespoon vegetable oil, for frying

Sour cream, for serving (optional)

MAKE THE APPLESAUCE

Add all of the ingredients to a medium-sized, heavy saucepan; stir, then bring to a boil over high heat. Boil, stirring occasionally, until the apples become very soft, about 10 minutes. Mash with a potato masher and set aside.

MAKE THE LATKES

1. Place the grated potatoes and onions on a large, clean kitchen towel. Gather the sides into the middle, roll up the towel, and squeeze the mixture over the sink to remove any excess liquid. Transfer the grated, drained potato-onion mixture to a large bowl, and stir in the Cheddar, flour, eggs, salt, and pepper.

2. Heat ¼ cup of the oil in a 10-inch, heavy, nonstick sauté pan over medium heat. When the oil is hot, add five ¼-cupfuls of the batter, flattening each circle a bit with a nonstick spatula. Cook until the first side is golden brown and crisp, about 3½ minutes. Flip and cook the other side until also golden brown and crisp, about another 3½ minutes. Transfer the finished latkes to a paper towel–lined baking sheet. Repeat with the remaining latke batter, not letting the pan go dry (you'll probably only need another 1 tablespoon oil).

TO SERVE

Serve the latkes with the applesauce and sour cream, if desired.

SERVING SUGGESTION: The latkes are also delicious as an appetizer or finger food at a party.

PB&J French Toast

Since this decadent breakfast recipe is fairly elemental, use high-quality ingredients: preserves, such as raspberry or strawberry (I love Bonne Maman® or Sarabeth's®); peanut butter (almond or cashew would also be delicious); and brioche. Also consider serving this dish for dessert, topped with vanilla ice cream or crème fraîche.

2 cups whole milk

5 large eggs

3 tablespoons light brown sugar

2 teaspoons pure vanilla extract

1 teaspoon ground cinnamon

½ teaspoon coarse salt

Eight ¾-inch-thick slices brioche or challah bread

4 tablespoons (½ stick) unsalted butter, for cooking the French toast

⅔ cup raspberry preserves

⅔ cup creamy peanut butter

1 tablespoon honey

Confectioners' sugar, for garnish

Fresh raspberries, for garnish

1. In a large baking dish, whisk together the milk, eggs, brown sugar, vanilla extract, cinnamon, and salt until well blended. Using tongs, soak each bread slice in the custard mixture for about 10 seconds per side, and then transfer to a plate.

2. Heat half of the butter over medium heat in a 10-inch non-stick frying pan. When the butter has melted, add four of the bread slices and cook until one side is golden brown, about 3 minutes. Turn and cook the remaining side until it is also golden brown, another 2 or 3 minutes. Transfer to a clean plate and repeat with the remaining butter and bread.

3. Just before cooking the second batch of French toast, pour the raspberry preserves and 2 tablespoons water into a small, heavy saucepan and heat over medium low until thinned out, 4 to 5 minutes. Place the peanut butter in a small microwave-safe bowl and microwave on high until thinned out a bit, stirring halfway through (this should take 20 to 45 seconds, depending on your microwave's strength). Stir in the honey.

4. Onto each serving plate, place one piece of French toast. Spread with some of the peanut butter mixture and drizzle on some of the raspberry mixture. Top with another piece of French toast, arranging it on a bit of an angle. Using a small handheld strainer or sifter, sprinkle the top of the French toast sandwich with some confectioners' sugar. Drizzle generously with more raspberry sauce. Strew some fresh raspberries all over the plate. Repeat with the remaining three portions, and serve.

SERVING SUGGESTION: Pour a big glass of ice cold milk!

Cheddar-Pecan Scones with Spiced Apple Butter

Savory and sophisticated, these scones pair beautifully with the spiced apple butter. After all, nutty and salty Cheddar, rich pecans, and sweet, crisp apples balance each other out and are frequently served together. Feel free to vary the shape and size of the scones.

1½ cups unbleached all-purpose flour, plus an extra 1 to 2 tablespoons for rolling out the dough

1 tablespoon plus 2 teaspoons granulated sugar, divided

1 tablespoon baking powder

½ teaspoon coarse salt

¼ teaspoon baking soda

5 tablespoons (½ stick plus 1 tablespoon) unsalted cold butter, diced

½ cup grated sharp Cheddar

½ cup finely chopped toasted pecans

About ½ cup plus 2 tablespoons buttermilk, cold and well-shaken

1 tablespoon 2% milk

MAKE THE SCONES

1. Heat the oven to 400°F and place a rack in the center of the oven. Line a baking sheet with parchment. In a medium-sized bowl, whisk together the 1½ cups flour, 1 tablespoon plus 1 teaspoon sugar, the baking powder, salt, and baking soda until well combined. Add the butter, cheese, and pecans, and, with your hands, quickly crumble the ingredients together until the dough is the size of small peas. Add the ½ cup of the buttermilk and use your hands to briefly and very gently knead it to form a ball of soft and sticky dough (do not over-mix). If the dough doesn't yet come together, add the remaining 2 tablespoons of buttermilk.

2. Sprinkle about 1 tablespoon flour onto a large, clean cold surface, and place the dough on top of it. Use your hands to pat the dough until it's ½ to ¾ inch thick. Use a 2-inch round biscuit cutter to cut out 6 scone rounds (combine any dough scraps). Brush with the milk and sprinkle evenly with the remaining 1 teaspoon of sugar. Transfer to the prepared baking sheet. Bake until cooked through and lightly golden brown on the bottom, about 20 minutes (carefully lift up a scone to check its bottom). Cool for about 5 minutes, and serve immediately with the apple butter.

SPICED APPLE BUTTER

8 tart apples, preferably Granny Smith, peeled, cored, and cut into large chunks

2 cups apple cider

¼ cup light brown sugar

1 teaspoon ground cinnamon

½ teaspoon coarse salt

¼ teaspoon ground cloves

¼ teaspoon ground allspice

MAKE THE APPLE BUTTER

Heat the oven to 400°F. Spray a 9 x 13 x 2-inch glass baking dish with cooking spray. Pour all of the ingredients into a large bowl and mix well. Pour into the baking dish, and bake, uncovered, until the apples are tender when pierced with a fork, about 35 minutes. Mash with a potato masher. Lower the oven temperature to 350°F, and continue to bake, stirring once in a while, until the apple mixture has formed a very thick, spreadable consistency, about 2 hours. Mash again with the potato masher (or purée with an immersion blender for a very smooth consistency), let cool a bit, and serve with the scones. Keep in the fridge, covered, for 1 week.

SERVING SUGGESTIONS: Serve the scones solo or, for a hearty country breakfast, alongside vegetarian sausage and eggs. Or, slice them open and fill with vegetarian bacon—with apple butter on the side! The scones are also delicious alongside the Veggie Chili with Butternut Squash on p. 117 or Scrambled Eggs with Chives and Mushroom-Maple Bundles on p. 21.

TRY THIS: Substitute walnuts for the pecans and serve with berry preserves if you don't have time to make the apple butter.

Roasted Two-Potato Hash with Poached Eggs

SERVES 4

The molten yolks of poached eggs supply the sauce over this flavorful, earthy hash. As savory as its meat counterpart, the hash (and eggs) would be delicious served with warm biscuits and fruit salad. If you prefer your yolks cooked all the way through and love crispy edges, go with fried eggs. This is also a great recipe for the brunch table.

1¾ pounds small waxy potatoes cut into 1- to 1½-inch pieces

10 ounces white button mushrooms, coarsely chopped

3 cups ½-inch dice peeled yams or sweet potatoes

¼ cup finely chopped red onions

¼ cup thinly sliced scallions, white and light green parts only

3 tablespoons tomato paste

3 tablespoons unsalted butter, melted (and still hot)

2 tablespoons vegetable oil

2 teaspoons seeded minced jalapeño

4 whole peeled garlic cloves

1 tablespoon plus 1¾ teaspoons coarse salt, divided

16 grinds black pepper, divided

¼ cup minced fresh chives

1 tablespoon white vinegar

8 large eggs, preferably fresh

1. Position an oven rack in the lower third of the oven, and heat the oven to 450°F. Line a baking sheet with aluminum foil, and spray with nonstick cooking spray. In a very large bowl, gently and thoroughly stir together the potatoes, mushrooms, yams, onions, scallions, tomato paste, hot melted butter, oil, jalapeño, garlic, 1½ teaspoons salt, and 8 grinds pepper. Pour onto the foil and spread evenly in one layer. Roast, stirring twice, until the potatoes are tender and very golden, 20 to 25 minutes (more than that and the small aromatics will begin to burn, so watch carefully). If desired, carefully remove and discard the garlic. Mix in the chives.

2. Meanwhile, fill a 10-inch, heavy Dutch oven halfway with water, and add 1 tablespoon salt and the vinegar. Cover and bring to a strong simmer over medium-high heat, then uncover and reduce the heat to medium low to achieve a very low simmer (with just a few small, gentle bubbles visible). Carefully crack an egg into a small cup, and then gently pour it into the water. Repeat with another 3 eggs, spacing them apart. Cook until the whites are opaque and set and the yolks bounce back just a tad when you lightly push them, 3½ to 4 minutes (depending on how molten you like the yolks). Use a spider or slotted spoon to transfer the poached eggs to a paper towel–lined baking sheet to drain. Poach the remaining 4 eggs. If desired, use kitchen shears to cut the egg whites into perfect ovals to neaten the presentation.

3. Divide the vegetable hash between four plates, and top each serving with 2 poached eggs. Sprinkle each pair of eggs with just a few grains of salt and 2 grinds of pepper. Serve.

Parfaits with Honey-Nut Granola, Greek Yogurt, and Fresh Berries

SERVES 6

This recipe (make it vegan by using soy or coconut milk yogurt) yields a gorgeous, family-style parfait or six individual parfaits. The granola will lose its crunch as it sits in the parfait, so make this shortly before serving. Keep the leftover granola in an airtight container and store at room temperature for up to a month.

½ cup plus 2 tablespoons extra-virgin olive oil

½ cup plus 2 tablespoons honey, divided

¼ cup plus 2 tablespoons dark brown sugar

2 cups old-fashioned rolled oats

1½ cups raw almonds (with skins), finely chopped

1 cup raw, hulled pumpkin seeds

1 cup sesame seeds

1¼ teaspoons coarse salt

1 teaspoon pure vanilla extract

1 teaspoon ground cinnamon

1 cup sweetened dried cherries

6 cups mixed fresh berries

1½ quarts 2% plain Greek yogurt

1. Heat the oven to 300°F. In a large bowl, whisk together the oil, ½ cup of the honey, and the dark brown sugar. Add the oats, almonds, pumpkin seeds, sesame seeds, salt, vanilla extract, and cinnamon and stir well. Line a baking sheet with sides with aluminum foil and grease the foil with nonstick cooking spray. Pour the oat-nut mixture onto the foil. Bake, stirring every 10 minutes, until the mixture is crisp and golden, about 55 minutes (watch it carefully so it doesn't burn). Pour the dried cherries onto the granola, and mix well. Let cool to room temperature, about 30 minutes (the granola will crisp up as it cools).

2. Meanwhile, in a medium bowl, mix the berries with the remaining 2 tablespoons of honey.

3. To serve family-style, spoon half of the yogurt into a large trifle dish, spreading it out to flatten. Top with 1 cup of granola, sprinkling it evenly, and half of the berries. Top with the remaining yogurt, flattening it out; add another cup of granola and spread it out; finally, top with the remaining berries. Serve, arranging individual parfait glasses alongside, for your guests to help themselves. If you're serving as individual parfaits, spoon equal amounts of yogurt, granola, and berries into six parfait glasses in layers, as directed for the trifle dish.

SERVING SUGGESTION: The parfait is dessert-like, so serve it with a savory dish, such as a vegetable frittata or eggs scrambled with fresh tarragon and chives.

Baklava Sticky Buns with Pistachios and Dates

SERVES 6; MAKES 12 SMALL BUNS

Sticky buns meet baklava in these decadent nut-capped treats. Serve them with lots of strong coffee or fresh-squeezed orange juice. Look for orange flower water in international, Mideastern, and gourmet stores. If you can't find it, substitute another tablespoon of orange juice.

½ cup warm (100°–110°F) 2% milk

One ¼-ounce packet active dry yeast

⅓ cup plus ½ teaspoon granulated sugar, divided

10 tablespoons (1 stick plus 2 tablespoons) unsalted butter, 4 tablespoons melted and the remainder at room temperature, divided

1 heaping teaspoon orange zest

1 teaspoon lemon zest

½ teaspoon plus ⅛ teaspoon coarse salt, divided

1 large egg, beaten

2¼ cups plus 1 tablespoon unbleached all-purpose flour, divided, plus more for the pan

⅔ packed cup plus 2 teaspoons dark brown sugar, divided

½ cup maple syrup

¼ cup fresh-squeezed, strained orange juice

2 tablespoons orange flower water

continued

1. In a small bowl, mix the warm milk, yeast, and ½ teaspoon granulated sugar. Let it sit until lots of small bubbles form, about 12 minutes. Meanwhile, combine the remaining ⅓ cup granulated sugar, ½ stick of the room temperature butter, the orange and lemon zests, and ½ teaspoon salt in a large bowl. Using an electric mixer with the paddle attachment, beat on medium speed until the mixture is well blended, light, and fluffy, about 3 minutes. Add the egg and beat for about 20 seconds, then add the yeast mixture and beat for about another 20 seconds.

2. Beat in 2 cups of the flour in three installments, beating for about 10 seconds after each addition and scraping down the sides of the bowl with a rubber spatula. Sprinkle about ¼ cup of the remaining flour onto a large clean surface; transfer the dough to the surface and knead until it's smooth and stretchy, about 4 minutes (add more flour if needed). Grease a large bowl with 1 tablespoon of the melted butter. Add the dough and turn to coat. Cover with plastic wrap and let rise in a warm place until doubled in volume, about 2 hours.

3. Meanwhile, grease the entire interior of a 9-inch round cake pan with 1 tablespoon of the melted butter. In a medium bowl, stir together the remaining 2 tablespoons melted butter, ⅔ cup of the brown sugar, the maple syrup, juice, and orange flower water. Pour this mixture into the bottom of the pan, and sprinkle evenly with the nuts.

continued

½ cup finely chopped raw
shelled pistachios

1 teaspoon ground cinnamon

½ teaspoon ground cardamom

1 cup coarsely chopped pitted
Medjool dates

4. Punch down the dough. Sprinkle the remaining 1 table-spoon flour onto a large clean work surface. Gently stretch the dough into a rectangle roughly 12 x 8 inches. Brush any excess flour off of the dough and spread the dough evenly with the remaining 2 tablespoons of room temperature butter. Mix the remaining 2 teaspoons brown sugar, the cinnamon, cardamom, and remaining ⅛ teaspoon salt in a small bowl. Sprinkle it evenly over the dough. Sprinkle the dates evenly on top.

5. Starting at one long side, tightly roll the dough into a log, keeping it as even as possible. Using a sharp knife, cut it into 12 rounds. (Spray the knife blade with nonstick cooking spray if it sticks to the dough as you cut it.) Place the rounds cut side down on top of the nuts in the pan. Cover the pan with plastic wrap and let the buns rise in a warm area until they double in volume, about 1 hour. Place a rack in the center of the oven, and heat the oven to 350°F.

6. Bake the buns on the center rack until they're golden brown on top and the insides are cooked through, 30 to 35 minutes (start checking after 25 minutes). Let cool in the pan for about 10 minutes, and then flip onto a serving plate. Cool for another 5 minutes and serve warm.

SERVING SUGGESTION: For a brunch buffet or elaborate meal, serve with warm flatbread, scrambled eggs, tomato and cucumber salad, and labneh (Mideastern strained yogurt).

TRY THIS: Dry yeast, which is dormant, dissolves and comes back to life when stirred into warm liquid, so you need to make sure the milk is sufficiently warm to activate the yeast. The liquid should feel warm, but not hot (if it's too hot, it can kill the yeast). To be sure, use an instant-read thermometer to check the temperature.

Strawberry-Vanilla Risotto

SERVES 4

This sweet take on a savory Italian classic is creamy, fruity, and needs no accompaniments. Use a combination of berry preserves (strawberry, raspberry, and sour cherry, for instance) for a more complex dish. Although you might use as little as 7½ cups of warm milk, heat up 9 cups, just in case you need more. To convert this dish to vegan, use trans-fat-free margarine and soy milk.

7½ to 9 cups 2% milk

4 tablespoons (½ stick) unsalted butter

1 teaspoon ground cinnamon

2 cups arborio rice (or other white risotto rice)

½ teaspoon coarse salt

2 cups hulled and quartered fresh strawberries, divided

½ cup high-quality strawberry preserves

2 teaspoons pure vanilla extract

1. In a large, heavy saucepan, bring the milk to a simmer over medium-high heat; immediately reduce the heat to low to keep warm.

2. Melt the butter in a 10-inch heavy sauté pan with at least 2-inch-high sides over medium heat. Add the cinnamon and stir for 1 minute. Add the rice and stir constantly for 2 minutes. Stir in the salt and ladle in about ¾ cup of the warm milk. Reduce the heat to medium low and simmer, stirring constantly. When only a tablespoon or two of liquid remains in the pan, add another ¾ cup of milk. Keep stirring and adding more warm milk until the risotto is soft and cooked through but still has a very faint bite to it, 25 to 30 minutes.

3. Stir in half of the strawberries, the preserves, and vanilla. Divide the risotto between four bowls, and top with the remaining strawberries. Serve immediately.

lunch & light entrées

GREEK SALAD WITH ROASTED SPICED CHICKPEAS AND WATERMELON. Egg salad tartines with fresh radish, basil, and watercress. Creamy Mexican carrot soup with black bean toasts. These are not your standard salads, sandwiches, and soups. Meet the ALT sandwich (avocado, lettuce, and tomato, that is), where baked Parmigiano-Reggiano rounds stand in for bacon. Or try the quinoa-polenta cakes with roasted red pepper sauce and white bean purée. Salty pecorino and fresh herbs perk up crisp zucchini fritters, while phyllo dough napoleons brim with pesto, creamy ricotta, and colorful summer vegetables. You'll also find versions of too-delicious-to-neglect classics, like tomato and mozzarella panini, Caesar salad, and leek and mushroom quiche.

Caesar Salad with Roasted Mushrooms, Garlic Croutons, and Creamy Chive Dressing

SERVES 4, WITH 2 CUPS DRESSING

In this recipe, soy sauce takes the place of the traditional anchovies, while silken tofu and olive oil stand in for raw eggs in the fresh chive-laced Caesar dressing. A combination of soy sauce, tomato paste, and mustard lend the tender roasted mushrooms a savory, meaty flavor (they'd also be a delicious antipasto on their own, if left in their marinade). ¶ To make this recipe vegan, omit the cheese from the salad dressing; just stir in some salt and a tad of sugar. ¶ The dressing makes double what you need for this recipe; save the remainder for another use. For ease, prepare the croutons and mushrooms a day ahead of time.

1¼ cups extra-virgin olive oil, divided

¼ cup plus 2 tablespoons red-wine vinegar, divided

3 tablespoons Dijon mustard, divided

2 tablespoons plus 1 teaspoon reduced-sodium soy sauce, divided

2 tablespoons tomato paste

1 tablespoon plus 1 teaspoon fresh thyme leaves (stems removed)

1 tablespoon granulated sugar

2 teaspoons coarse salt, divided

About ½ teaspoon black pepper, divided

½ pound shiitake mushrooms, stems removed and discarded and caps cut into 1-inch pieces

1. Heat the oven to 400°F. On a baking sheet with sides, mix together ½ cup olive oil, ¼ cup vinegar, 2 tablespoons mustard, 2 tablespoons soy sauce, all of the tomato paste, all of the fresh thyme, all of the sugar, 1 teaspoon salt, and a pinch of pepper. Add the mushrooms and use your hands to coat thoroughly in the marinade. Once the oven is hot, roast until warm and tender, about 15 minutes. Pour into a colander set in the sink to drain, discarding any leftover marinade (reserve the mushrooms).

2. Lower the oven temperature to 350°F. On another baking sheet with sides, toss together another ¼ cup olive oil, all of the bread cubes, the three finely chopped garlic cloves (about 1 tablespoon plus ½ teaspoon), ½ teaspoon salt, and a pinch of pepper. Bake until crisp and golden brown, about 15 minutes, shaking the pan halfway through. Immediately pour the croutons onto a cool surface, so the garlic stops cooking; set aside to cool.

1 pound portabella mushrooms, stems removed and discarded and caps cut into 1-inch pieces

5 cups 1-inch cubes country bread

5 garlic cloves, 3 of them finely chopped, divided

½ pound silken tofu

¼ cup coarsely chopped fresh chives

2 tablespoons fresh-squeezed, strained lemon juice

1 cup freshly grated Parmigiano-Reggiano

Scant 1 pound romaine heart leaves, washed and spun dry, and torn into bite-sized pieces

2 cups cherry tomatoes, halved

3. Add the remaining 2 whole cloves garlic to a food processor. Process until finely chopped, about 5 seconds. Add the tofu, chives, the remaining 1 tablespoon mustard, the remaining 2 tablespoons vinegar, all of the lemon juice, the remaining 1 teaspoon of the soy sauce, and a small pinch of pepper. Process until smooth, about 10 seconds. Add the remaining ½ cup olive oil and process until well blended, about 5 seconds. Stir in the cheese, and set the dressing aside.

4. In a large bowl, toss together the lettuce, halved tomatoes, the remaining ½ teaspoon salt and the remaining 10 grinds pepper. Pour in 1 cup of the dressing and toss again. Using the tongs, divide the salad among four plates. Onto each plate, spoon ½ cup of the croutons and ¼ cup plus 2 tablespoons of the roasted mushrooms. Serve.

SERVING SUGGESTION: Cap off the meal with poached apricots drizzled in caramel sauce.

TRY THIS: To guarantee a delicious salad, dry the greens well, using a salad spinner. Cover the greens with a couple of paper towels in the salad spinner, transfer to the refrigerator, and let them chill and dry out for at least an hour.

Black Bean Burgers with Grilled Mango-Lime Mayonnaise

SERVES 4

This vegan entrée features black bean burgers topped with a fruity mango mayonnaise, crunchy red onions, fresh arugula, and a juicy tomato slice. The recipe makes four 4-ounce burgers, the ideal size for lunch. If you're making the burgers for dinner and are after a heartier serving, simply double the burger portion of the recipe (the mayonnaise makes enough for 12 burgers).

1 large, juicy lime, zested and juiced (juice strained), divided

3 tablespoons canola oil, divided; more for the pan

1 large ripe mango, peeled and cut into ⅓-inch-thick slices

1½ teaspoons coarse salt, divided

Scant ⅓ teaspoon black pepper, divided

½ cup vegan mayonnaise

¼ cup fresh cilantro or flat-leaf parsley leaves

One 15-ounce can black beans, rinsed and drained

1 cup panko breadcrumbs

¼ cup ketchup

1 medium red onion, ¼ cup finely chopped and the remainder cut into rings, divided

1 teaspoon yellow mustard

½ teaspoon Sriracha or hot sauce

4 burger buns

1 small, ripe tomato, sliced thinly

About 1 cup arugula leaves, washed and spun dry

1. In a small bowl, whisk together 1 tablespoon lime juice with 1 tablespoon oil. Dip both sides of the mango slices in the marinade, and then arrange the fruit on a large surface (discard the marinade). Sprinkle both sides of the slices evenly with a total of ¼ teaspoon salt and a bit of pepper.

2. Heat a grill pan over medium-high heat and brush with oil. When hot, carefully add the marinated mango slices. Grill until char marks appear, about 5 minutes total, turning over halfway through. Turn off the grill. Remove the mango from the heat and let cool to room temperature, at least 15 minutes (don't worry if the mango breaks apart; you will be puréeing it anyway).

3. Once the mango is cool, blend it with the mayonnaise, cilantro, lime zest, 1 tablespoon lime juice, ¼ teaspoon salt, and a pinch of pepper in a food processor until smooth, about 20 seconds (you should yield 1½ cups). Set aside.

4. Clean out the food processor bowl. Add the black beans, panko, ketchup, chopped red onions, mustard, Sriracha, ¾ teaspoon salt, and a pinch of pepper. Pulse until the mixture comes together, about 30 seconds. Transfer to a clean work surface and briefly and gently knead together until the mixture is well blended.

5. Divide the black bean mixture into 4 portions and shape each one into a patty about ½ inch thick. Make an indentation in the center of each patty by pressing in with your fingers. Brush both sides of all of the patties with a total of 1 tablespoon oil, then sprinkle both sides evenly with a total of

¼ teaspoon salt and a bit of pepper. Open up each burger bun and brush the remaining 1 tablespoon oil on the interior surface of the 4 buns.

6. Brush the grill clean, and reheat to medium high. When hot, add the burgers and cook until grill marks appear on the first side, about 4 minutes. Carefully flip and cook until grill marks appear on the second side, another 3 to 4 minutes; remove from the heat. Grill the buns, oiled sides down, until grill marks appear, about 2 minutes.

7. Place a patty on half of each grilled bun. Divide the red onion rings, tomato slices, and arugula among the patties; spread the top half of the buns with about 2 tablespoons of the mayonnaise. Serve.

SERVING SUGGESTIONS: Pair the burgers with coleslaw, and finish your meal with chilled coconut rice pudding topped with sliced mango.

TRY THIS: Vary this recipe by using another type of canned bean, such as pinto. If you're short on time, skip grilling the mango and instead dice 1 ripe mango and add to the food processor with the other mayo ingredients.

Banh Mi Sandwiches with Tempeh

SERVES 4

These vegan Vietnamese-inspired sandwiches are full of crunch, with a sweet-tart flavor. Make sure to choose a fresh baguette that's not too skinny and to slice the carrots very thinly. Feel free to substitute thinly sliced daikon radish for half of the carrots and extra-firm tofu for the tempeh (both tofu and tempeh can be found in the refrigerated section of the supermarket).

¼ cup black bean sauce with garlic

2 tablespoons toasted sesame oil

¼ cup plus 1 tablespoon unseasoned rice vinegar, divided

2 teaspoons agave nectar

One 8-ounce package unflavored tempeh, sliced ¼ inch thick

2 tablespoons canola oil

1 tablespoon plus ½ teaspoon granulated sugar

¼ teaspoon coarse salt

5 grinds black pepper

1 cup very thinly sliced (on the bias) carrots

1 cup thinly sliced (on the bias) English cucumbers

One 1-pound baguette, ends cut off and the remainder sliced in half lengthwise

continued

1. Heat the oven to 300°F. In a baking dish, whisk together the black bean sauce, sesame oil, 1 tablespoon rice vinegar, and all of the agave nectar. Add the tempeh slices and gently toss with your fingers to coat all sides. Let marinate at room temperature for 20 minutes.

2. Heat the oil over medium high in a 12-inch, heavy, nonstick, frying pan. When the oil is hot, add the marinated tempeh and cook for 2 minutes on the first side. Use a spatula to gently flip, and cook the remaining side for 2 minutes. Remove from the heat and set aside.

3. Meanwhile, in a small bowl, whisk together the remaining ¼ cup rice vinegar, all of the sugar, all of the salt, and the black pepper. Add the carrots and cucumbers, and let marinate for 20 minutes at room temperature (not much longer or the cucumbers will lose their texture). Place a colander over a large bowl and pour the pickled vegetables into the colander (discard the pickling liquid and reserve the pickles).

continued

½ cup vegan mayonnaise

½ cup very thinly sliced red onions

3 tablespoons thinly sliced jalapeño (flesh only, no seeds or membranes)

½ heaping packed cup fresh cilantro leaves

4. Use your fingers to pull out (and discard) some of the insides from both halves of the baguette (this is to slightly thin out the bread to establish the ideal filling-to-bread ratio). Wrap the baguette tightly in foil and transfer to the oven to warm, about 5 minutes.

5. Evenly slather the mayonnaise on the bottom half of the warm baguette. Sprinkle evenly with the red onions and jalapeño. Evenly arrange the tempeh on top, then the drained pickled cucumbers, then the drained pickled carrots, and finally the fresh cilantro. Top with the other bread half; cut into 4 pieces and serve.

SERVING SUGGESTION: Since the sandwiches are a meal in themselves, they need no accompaniments other than iced lychees for dessert.

TRY THIS: For extra heat, add Sriracha sauce to the vegan mayonnaise.

Grilled Cheese with Apples, Mustard, and Cheddar

SERVES 4

Loaded with rich and creamy Cheddar; slightly crisp, sweet apples; and pungent mustard and horseradish, these grilled cheese sandwiches are truly special. With such a simple sandwich, it's important to use the best ingredients and to watch carefully as they cook. I usually switch the stovetop heat levels between medium and low in the process. The goal is crisp, golden brown bread and melted cheese.

1 tablespoon plus 1 teaspoon Dijon mustard

One 1-pound loaf unsliced high-quality white or wheat bread, cut into 8 roughly ½-inch-thick slices

1 teaspoon prepared white horseradish, drained

5 ounces sharp Cheddar, grated

1 Granny Smith apple, cored, halved vertically, and very thinly sliced into 28 slices

⅛ teaspoon coarse salt

4 grinds black pepper

4 tablespoons (½ stick) unsalted butter, divided

1. Spread the mustard evenly on 4 slices of bread. Spread the horseradish evenly on the other 4 slices of bread. Arrange the cheese and apple slices on top of the bread slices with mustard. Sprinkle the salt and pepper evenly on the apples. Top with the remaining 4 slices of bread, with their horseradish sides facing down.

2. Heat half of the butter in a 10-inch, heavy, nonstick sauté pan over medium heat. Once the butter has melted, add two sandwiches and press down firmly with your hand. Cook until the first side turns golden brown, about 4 minutes. Carefully flip and cook until the other side is golden brown, about 4 minutes. Cover with a lid and reduce the heat to medium low. Cook until the cheese has melted, about 2 minutes (watch carefully to prevent burning; you might need to reduce the heat to low). Transfer to a cutting board.

3. Add the remaining butter and the remaining two sandwiches and repeat the cooking process, which should take about 2 minutes less this time around. Cut all of the sandwiches in half and serve immediately.

SERVING SUGGESTIONS: Serve these sandwiches with beer and a red cabbage and apple slaw. Try chocolate pudding for dessert.

Quartet of Tea Sandwiches

This meal—a vegetarian take on afternoon tea sandwiches—is so satisfying that even carnivores won't miss the traditional chicken salad or smoked salmon filling. Begin with the cucumber-radish sandwiches with dill cream cheese, and progress to the sun-dried tomato and watercress. Next, try the Cheddar and chutney, and finish with the date and lemon cream cheese (the recipe makes four different sandwiches per person). ❡ To simplify meal preparation, remove the cream cheese and goat cheese from the fridge first so they have time to soften. Use a large white platter for serving the sandwiches, and arrange them in the above order—from the most savory to the most sweet.

One 24-ounce loaf high-quality unsliced white or whole wheat bread (not multigrain)

8 very thin slices English cucumber

12 very thin slices radish

About ½ teaspoon coarse salt, divided

4 ounces cream cheese, at room temperature, divided

2 teaspoons finely chopped fresh dill

1 scant teaspoon lemon zest

8 pitted dates, pressed flat

2 teaspoons finely chopped, skinned toasted hazelnuts, at room temperature

2 ounces fresh goat cheese, at room temperature

1. Using a sharp serrated knife, cut the crusts and edges off all sides of the bread loaf, leaving a white rectangle with sharp edges. Slice the rectangle into 16 slices. Cut each slice into 2 triangles, for a total of 32 triangles (for 16 sandwiches).

2. Place the cucumber and radish slices in a small bowl of ice water. Let sit for a few minutes, then drain well and line up on a clean, dry dishtowel. Sprinkle evenly with a total of a scant ⅛ teaspoon of the salt.

3. Evenly divide the cream cheese into two small bowls. Stir ⅛ teaspoon salt and all of the dill into one of the bowls and mix well. Spread the dill cream cheese on 4 bread triangles. Arrange 2 slices of the drained cucumbers and 3 slices of the drained radishes on top. Top with another 4 triangles of bread, and place the finished sandwiches on the platter.

4. Add ⅛ teaspoon salt and the lemon zest to the other bowl of cream cheese and mix well. Spread the lemon cream cheese on 4 bread triangles. Top each with 2 dates and ½ teaspoon hazelnuts. Place 4 other bread triangles on top, and place the finished sandwiches on the platter.

2 tablespoons watercress leaves, washed and dried

8 sun-dried tomatoes packed in oil, drained well on paper towels

1 teaspoon Dijon mustard

2 ounces sharp Cheddar, cut into four triangles (that will fit on a bread triangle)

1 tablespoon high-quality mango chutney, such as Geeta's®

5. In a small bowl, mix together the goat cheese and ⅛ teaspoon salt. Spread on 4 bread triangles. Place ½ tablespoon watercress leaves and 2 sun-dried tomatoes on top of the goat cheese. Top with 4 bread triangles, and place the finished sandwiches on the platter.

6. Divide the mustard among 4 bread triangles. Top each with a triangle of Cheddar and one-quarter of the chutney. Top with the remaining 4 bread triangles. Place the finished sandwiches on the platter, and serve.

SERVING SUGGESTIONS: Brew a large pot of black tea and whip up a lightly dressed green salad and a fruit salad to serve with the sandwiches.

TRY THIS: Be creative—or traditional—with other fillings. Consider egg salad; smoked mozzarella, pesto, and sun-dried tomato; cashew butter and apricot preserves; and chocolate-hazelnut spread with dried apricots.

Roasted Root Vegetable and Goat Cheese Salad with Lemon-Tahini Vinaigrette

SERVES 4

This Mideastern-inspired salad makes a beautiful fall or winter lunch. To make the dish vegan, omit the goat cheese or substitute a vegan cheese.

16 small (two-bite) potatoes, ideally in several colors, quartered

¾ cup plus 1 tablespoon extra-virgin olive oil, divided

1⅛ teaspoons salt, divided

14 grinds black pepper, divided

½ large head cauliflower, cut into ½-inch florets

3 small carrots, peeled and cut into ⅓-inch-thick matchsticks

½ large parsnip, trimmed, peeled, starchy core cut out, and the remainder cut into ⅓-inch-thick matchsticks

1 small clove garlic

¼ cup plus 1 tablespoon fresh-squeezed, strained lemon juice

1¼ cups fresh flat-leaf parsley leaves, divided

1 tablespoon tahini (sesame seed paste), well mixed

1 teaspoon honey

⅛ teaspoon ground cumin

⅛ teaspoon ground coriander

continued

1. Heat the oven to 400°F. Add the potatoes, 2 tablespoons oil, ¼ teaspoon salt, and 4 grinds pepper to a baking sheet with sides. Use your hands to mix well and spread out in one layer. Bake until tender and golden brown, about 30 minutes.

2. Meanwhile, on another baking sheet with sides, place the cauliflower, 1 tablespoon oil, ¼ teaspoon salt, and 4 grinds pepper. Use your hands to toss well, and spread out in one layer on half of the pan. On the other half of that same pan, place the carrots, parsnips, 2 tablespoons oil, ¼ teaspoon salt, and 4 grinds pepper. Use your hands to mix well, and spread out in one layer. Keep the carrot-parsnip mixture separate from the cauliflower. Roast the vegetables until tender and slightly golden brown, about 20 minutes. Let the vegetables cool off the heat.

3. While the vegetables are roasting, process the garlic in a food processor until minced, about 5 seconds. Add the remaining ½ cup olive oil, ¼ teaspoon salt, 2 grinds pepper, all of the lemon juice, ¼ cup parsley, the tahini, honey, cumin, and coriander; process until smooth, about 20 seconds. Set aside (you should have a generous ¾ cup).

continued

About ⅔ head green leaf
lettuce, cored, outer leaves
removed and discarded, and
the remainder sliced into
bite-sized pieces, washed,
and spun dry

1 cup coarsely chopped fresh
dill

4 ounces fresh goat cheese,
crumbled

4. In a large bowl, toss together the remaining 1 cup parsley, the
lettuce, dill, and the remaining ⅛ teaspoon salt. With tongs,
place a quarter of the lettuce mixture on one plate. Top with
one-quarter each of the potatoes, cauliflower, carrot-parsnip
mixture, and goat cheese. Drizzle 3 tablespoons of the dressing over the top. Repeat with the remaining three plates
and serve.

SERVING SUGGESTIONS: Serve slices of whole wheat
baguette alongside. For dessert, offer a platter of fresh figs,
dates, clementines, and toasted almonds.

TRY THIS: Feel free to substitute other root vegetables.
Roast beets instead of parsnips (adjust the time so the beets
are cooked until tender). Also, use fresh cilantro or mint
leaves instead of the parsley or dill, and try fresh orange or
lime juice instead of lemon juice.

ALT Sandwiches with Frico

MAKES 4 SANDWICHES, WITH ABOUT 1¾ CUPS SPREAD

Ideal for summer, when tomatoes are at their peak, these avocado-lettuce-tomato sandwiches feature frico (baked Parmigiano-Reggiano rounds) instead of crispy, salty bacon. A white bean-avocado-basil spread is smooth, satisfying, and creamy (and pretty, too).

1 cup freshly grated Parmigiano-Reggiano

1 tablespoon unbleached all-purpose flour

2 garlic cloves

One 15-ounce can cannellini beans, rinsed and drained

Flesh of 1 ripe avocado

¾ cup fresh basil leaves (about 1 ounce fresh basil, including stems)

2 tablespoons fresh-squeezed, strained lemon juice (from 1 lemon)

2 tablespoons extra-virgin olive oil

1 teaspoon coarse salt, divided

5 grinds black pepper

8 slices sourdough or country bread, toasted

8 slices cored beefsteak tomato

8 to 12 leaves red leaf or romaine lettuce, washed and spun dry

1. Heat the oven to 375°F. Line a baking sheet with parchment. In a small bowl, mix together the cheese and flour. With a tablespoon measure, scoop out 10 tablespoons of the cheese-flour mixture onto the parchment, forming mounds spaced a few inches apart. Flatten each mound a bit into a circle.

2. Bake until the cheese has melted and the rounds are lightly golden brown, 10 to 12 minutes. Let cool on the baking sheet for 2 minutes, then remove the frico rounds from the parchment (use your fingers) and carefully transfer to a cool surface.

3. Put the garlic in a food processor and process until minced, about 8 seconds. Add the beans, avocado, basil, lemon juice, oil, ¾ teaspoon salt, and the pepper, and process until smooth, about another 40 seconds.

4. To make one sandwich, spoon about ¼ cup plus 2 tablespoons of the avocado spread on top of 1 slice of bread. Top with 2 tomato slices, sprinkling them evenly with a pinch of salt. Top with 2 or 3 lettuce leaves and then 2 or 3 cheese rounds. Place the other bread slice on top. Repeat with the remaining 3 sandwiches and serve immediately.

SERVING SUGGESTIONS: These Italian-inspired sandwiches would be delicious served with other jewels of summer: a fresh corn or green and wax bean salad and peach ice cream for dessert.

Tabbouleh with Dates and Pomegranate Vinaigrette

SERVES 4 TO 6

In this vibrant vegan dish—a cross between Mideastern tabbouleh and bazargan—I use bell pepper rather than tomato because the pepper holds up better. ¶ Sumac is a purple-red spice with a lemony flavor. It's available at Mideastern and other international markets, but omit it if you can't find it. If you use traditional cucumber in place of the English cucumber, peel and seed before chopping.

1 cup dried bulgur wheat

1½ teaspoons coarse salt, divided

¼ cup fresh-squeezed, strained lemon juice

¼ cup extra-virgin olive oil

2 tablespoons pomegranate molasses

2 tablespoons finely chopped shallots

1 tablespoon red-wine vinegar

¼ teaspoon ground cumin

¼ teaspoon ground coriander

¼ teaspoon sumac

⅛ teaspoon cayenne or Aleppo pepper

One 15-ounce can chickpeas, rinsed and drained

1½ cups finely chopped red bell peppers

1 cup finely chopped English cucumbers

1 cup shredded carrots

½ cup chopped pitted dates

½ cup finely chopped fresh flat-leaf parsley or cilantro leaves

¼ cup thinly sliced scallions, white and light green parts only

1. Bring 1½ cups of water to a boil. Add the bulgur and 1 teaspoon salt to a large bowl, and pour the boiling water on top. Cover and let sit until the bulgur is tender, about 30 minutes.

2. Meanwhile, in a medium bowl, whisk together the lemon juice, oil, pomegranate molasses, shallots, vinegar, cumin, coriander, sumac, cayenne, and ¼ teaspoon salt. Set aside.

3. Add the chickpeas, bell peppers, cucumbers, carrots, dates, parsley, scallions, and the remaining ¼ teaspoon salt to the bulgur. Add the dressing and mix well to combine. Serve.

SERVING SUGGESTIONS: Serve the salad with warm pita bread; follow it with halvah, baklava, or other traditional Mideastern sweets.

Edamame Hummus with Baked Feta and Warm Pita Bread

SERVES 4

Feel free to substitute thawed and drained frozen peas or fava beans for the edamame, and make sure to mix the tahini well before using.

About 12 ounces fresh feta

2 tablespoons extra-virgin olive oil

1 tablespoon fresh-squeezed, strained lemon juice

6 grinds black pepper

⅛ teaspoon Aleppo pepper or crushed red pepper flakes

Several sprigs fresh thyme

4 whole wheat pita breads

Edamame Hummus (recipe follows)

Heat the oven to 375°F. Place the feta in a small baking dish and top with the oil, lemon juice, black pepper, Aleppo pepper, and thyme. Bake until the cheese is soft and warm, about 30 minutes. Ten minutes after putting the cheese in the oven, wrap the pitas tightly in aluminum foil and place in the oven; heat for 20 minutes. Serve the warm cheese and pitas with the Edamame Hummus.

SERVING SUGGESTIONS: Serve this light Mediterranean meal with a chopped tomato and cucumber salad. The ideal dessert would be fresh figs with Greek yogurt, drizzled with honey and sprinkled with chopped pistachios.

TRY THIS: Host a Mideastern-themed party. In addition to the baked feta, hummus, and pita, set out olives, grape leaves, mini spinach pies, marinated roasted peppers, and toasted, seasoned pistachios.

EDAMAME HUMMUS

MAKES A SCANT 3 CUPS

2 large cloves garlic

One 1-pound bag frozen
blanched and shelled
edamame (soy beans), thawed
and drained

¼ cup packed fresh mint leaves

2 tablespoons tahini (sesame
seed paste)

2 tablespoons fresh-squeezed,
strained lemon juice

1 teaspoon coarse salt

¼ teaspoon cumin

¼ teaspoon coriander

⅛ teaspoon Aleppo pepper

5 grinds black pepper

1¼ cups extra-virgin olive oil

Add the garlic to the bowl of a food processor and process until finely chopped, about 5 seconds. Add all of the remaining ingredients except for the oil. Process until well mixed and relatively smooth, about 15 seconds. Add the oil and process until very smooth, about another 40 seconds; scrape down the sides of the bowl with a rubber spatula to make sure all of the ingredients are incorporated.

Egg Salad Tartines with Fresh Radish, Basil, and Watercress

SERVES 4

These colorful, fresh, open-face sandwiches are ideal for lunch or afternoon tea. Feel free to vary the herbs, substituting fresh tarragon, dill, or chervil for the chives.

12 large eggs

½ cup mayonnaise

¼ cup minced chives

¼ cup finely chopped shallots

1 tablespoon Dijon mustard

1 teaspoon lemon zest

½ teaspoon coarse salt

10 grinds black pepper

Four 1-inch-thick slices crusty pumpernickel or rye bread, toasted

32 basil leaves, washed and dried

4 radishes, trimmed and thinly sliced

1 cup watercress leaves, washed and dried

1. Place the eggs in a large saucepan and cover with about 2 inches of cold water. Cover and bring to a boil over high heat. As soon as the water comes to a full boil, remove the covered pan from the heat and set the timer for 12 minutes. Pour the hard-cooked eggs into a colander set in the sink. Immediately begin running cold water over the eggs and jostle them in the colander. Peel while the cold water continues to run over them.

2. Transfer the peeled eggs to a medium-sized bowl. Add the mayonnaise, chives, shallots, mustard, lemon zest, salt, and pepper. Mash the eggs with a potato masher, and mix the ingredients well with a large spoon (you should have about 3¼ cups salad).

3. Dollop a quarter of the egg salad onto each slice of bread and top with a quarter of the basil leaves, a quarter of the radishes, and a quarter of the watercress. Slice in half and serve.

SERVING SUGGESTIONS: Serve with fruit salad and iced tea, with strawberry tarts for dessert.

TRY THIS: If you like, dollop the salad onto cocktail bread slices, crackers, or croutes and serve as finger food or appetizers.

Poblano, Black Bean, and Corn Quesadillas with Guacamole

SERVES 4

I've been making quesadillas since my college days. After all, they're delicious, and quick and easy to prepare. Now that I have kids, I have even more reason to make them. Quesadillas are such a child-friendly treat: grilled cheese, but slightly more interesting! Opt for a soy cheese (I like Daiya™) to keep the recipe vegan.

2 poblano peppers

One 15-ounce can black beans, rinsed and drained

2 cups shredded pepper Jack cheese

1 cup frozen sweet yellow corn, thawed to room temperature and drained

¼ cup coarsely chopped fresh cilantro leaves, divided

1 teaspoon coarse salt, divided

⅛ teaspoon ancho chile powder

Flesh of 3 ripe avocados,

½ cup canned no-salt-added, fire-roasted diced tomatoes, drained (I like Muir Glen)

¼ cup finely chopped shallots

1 tablespoon fresh-squeezed strained lime juice

4 grinds black pepper

About ¼ cup vegetable oil, divided

Four 7-inch-diameter flour tortillas

1. Place each poblano directly on a gas burner, and turn each burner to high. Roast, turning occasionally with tongs, until blackened on all sides, about 10 minutes. (Alternatively, roast in the oven by placing the peppers on a baking sheet and cooking at 450°F, turning every 10 to 15 minutes, until fully charred, about 30 minutes.) Place the charred peppers on the countertop and cover completely with a large upside-down bowl; steam until tender, about 20 minutes.

2. Peel off and discard the black charred flesh. Slice open each pepper and discard the seeds and stem (doing this under running water can make seeding easier). Cut the pepper flesh into small dice. Place ½ cup of the diced peppers in a large bowl, and add the beans, cheese, corn, 2 tablespoons cilantro, ½ teaspoon salt, and the ancho chili powder. Stir well.

3. Place the avocado flesh in a medium bowl and mash with a potato masher. Add the drained tomatoes, shallots, the remaining 2 tablespoons cilantro, lime juice, the remaining ½ teaspoon salt, and the pepper. Stir well. Place a piece of plastic wrap directly on the surface to counteract browning. (The guacamole yields about 1¾ cups.)

4. Heat 1 tablespoon oil in each of two 10-inch nonstick frying pans over medium-high heat. When hot (but not smoking), add 1 tortilla to each pan. Cook on one side for 30 seconds,

then gently flip and reduce the heat to medium. After flipping, spoon a generous amount of black bean filling onto one half of each tortilla, spreading it out evenly. Fold over the remaining half of the tortilla and press down. Cook until the side facing down is golden brown, about 2 minutes. Very carefully (using tongs), flip the quesadilla, trying to keep the filling inside (nudge it back in if it oozes out). Cook until the side facing down is similarly golden brown and the cheese has melted, about another 2 minutes. Use a spatula to gently transfer the quesadillas to serving plates. Cover with foil to keep warm.

5. Turn off the heat and carefully wipe out the pans. Return the heat to medium and repeat the cooking process with the remaining 2 tortillas and filling, adding another 1 tablespoon oil to each pan. Serve the quesadillas with the guacamole.

SERVING SUGGESTIONS: Serve these hot Mexican grilled cheese sandwiches with a mango, radish, and jícama salad. For dessert, try fresh pineapple and watermelon sprinkled with lime juice, salt, and chile powder.

Grilled Cheese with Gruyère, Sautéed Mushrooms, and Oven-Roasted Tomatoes

SERVES 4

Sweet and juicy oven-roasted tomatoes, nutty Gruyère, and earthy shiitake mushrooms meet crisp country bread in these sophisticated grilled cheese sandwiches. Be sure to use a high-quality butter (such as Organic Valley® or Lurpak®), since you truly will taste it. For variation, you can add Dijon mustard or substitute grated Fontina for the Gruyère. You can also make the sandwiches a few minutes in advance, transfer them to a baking sheet, and keep them warm in a 300°F oven.

4 plum tomatoes, cored and halved lengthwise

1 tablespoon extra-virgin olive oil

1 tablespoon plus 1½ teaspoons minced garlic, divided

5 sprigs fresh thyme

½ teaspoon coarse salt, divided

12 grinds black pepper, divided

4 tablespoons (½ stick) unsalted butter, divided

3½ ounces shiitake mushrooms, stems removed and discarded and caps thinly sliced

Eight ½-inch-thick slices country bread from a large loaf, such as *pain de campagne* or sourdough

¼ cup plus 2 tablespoons mayonnaise

1⅓ cups packed shredded Gruyère

3 tablespoons vegetable oil, divided

1. Heat the oven to 275°F. Arrange the tomatoes cut side up on a baking sheet with sides. Drizzle with the olive oil and sprinkle evenly with 1 tablespoon garlic, the thyme, ¼ teaspoon salt, and 8 grinds pepper. Roast until halfway dried out, about 2 hours and 45 minutes. Set aside.

2. Heat 2 tablespoons of the butter in a 10-inch, heavy, non-stick sauté pan over medium-high heat. Once the butter has melted, add the remaining 1½ teaspoons garlic and sauté for 1 minute (no more, to prevent burning). Add the mushrooms, the remaining ¼ teaspoon salt, and 4 grinds pepper, and sauté until very tender, about 5 minutes. Set aside.

3. Arrange 4 bread slices on a work surface and sprinkle the cheese on top. Place the cooked mushrooms and oven-roasted tomatoes on top of the cheese (divide them evenly among the slices). Top with the remaining 4 slices of bread. Spread both outward-facing sides of the bread with the mayonnaise (divide it evenly among the slices).

4. Wipe out the 10-inch sauté pan. Heat the remaining 2 tablespoons butter and 1 tablespoon oil over medium heat. Once the butter has melted, add 2 sandwiches and cook until the first side is golden brown and crisp, about 5 minutes, pressing down on the sandwiches with a spatula. Carefully flip the sandwiches; cover the pan with a lid, and cook until the other side is similarly golden brown and crisp and the cheese has melted, about another 3 minutes (watch the pan; you might need to lower the heat to medium low). Transfer the sandwiches to a cutting board. Add the remaining 2 tablespoons oil and the remaining 2 sandwiches and cook as directed. Slice the sandwiches in half and serve immediately.

SERVING SUGGESTIONS: These sandwiches pair well with a crisp frisée salad with white beans and fennel; serve orange sorbet for dessert.

TRY THIS: To lighten up this decadent dish, skip the mayonnaise, cut down on the cheese, opt for whole wheat country bread, and cook the mushrooms in a small amount of olive oil.

Thai Salad with Crispy Tofu and Peanut Dressing

SERVES 4

This colorful one-dish meal features golden brown pan-fried tofu sticks, hard-cooked eggs, sweet and verdant snow peas, crispy lettuce, juicy red tomatoes, and a sweet and creamy peanut dressing. Omit the hard-cooked eggs to make the entrée vegan. ¶ Be sure to use a high-quality creamy peanut butter; I love Maranatha® No Stir Creamy Peanut Butter (which includes a bit of sugar and salt). If you use a different brand and your dressing isn't sweet or salty enough, adjust with a bit more dark brown sugar and soy sauce.

4 large eggs

About 1 teaspoon coarse salt, plus extra for salting the water, divided

About ¼ teaspoon black pepper, divided

14 ounces extra-firm tofu

1 cup snow peas, strings cut off

¼ cup plus 2 tablespoons minced shallots

¼ cup creamy peanut butter, at room temperature

¼ cup peanut oil, at room temperature

2 tablespoons unseasoned rice vinegar

2 tablespoons fresh-squeezed, strained lime juice

2 tablespoons dark brown sugar

2 tablespoons reduced-sodium soy sauce

⅓ cup unbleached all-purpose flour

¼ cup vegetable oil

continued

1. Place the eggs in a heavy medium saucepan and cover by about 2 inches with water; cover and bring to a full boil over high heat. Immediately move the pot to a cool burner. Cover the pot and set the timer for 12 minutes. Carefully pour the hard-cooked eggs into a colander set in the sink, then immediately run cold water over the eggs. Jostle the colander repeatedly to crack the shells, and peel the eggs under cold running water. Halve the eggs vertically and sprinkle them evenly with a total of ⅛ teaspoon salt and a pinch of the pepper.

2. Meanwhile, overlap three paper towels on a large plate. Place the block of tofu on top and top with another three overlapping paper towels and another large plate. Let sit for 30 minutes.

3. While the tofu is draining, fill a heavy small saucepan two-thirds full of heavily salted water, cover, and bring to a boil over high heat. Once boiling, uncover, add the snow peas, and boil until bright green and crisp-tender, about 3 minutes. Carefully pour them into a colander set in the sink; run cold water over the snow peas for a couple of minutes. Then drain and set aside.

continued

4 cups romaine lettuce leaves,
washed and spun dry and
torn into bite-sized pieces

1 cup shredded carrots

1 cup grape or cherry tomatoes

2 cups thinly sliced English
cucumbers

¼ cup unsalted peanuts,
lightly toasted and coarsely
chopped

4. In a medium bowl, whisk together the shallots, peanut butter, peanut oil, rice vinegar, lime juice, sugar, and soy sauce
(you should have about 1 cup of dressing). Set aside at room
temperature.

5. Slice the drained tofu into 12 equally sized sticks, each one
about ¾ inch. Line them up close together and sprinkle
both sides evenly with a total of ½ teaspoon salt and a pinch
of pepper. Pour the flour into a medium bowl. Dredge all
sides of each tofu stick in the flour, coating well and shaking
off the excess. Set the tofu aside.

6. Heat the vegetable oil over medium high in a 10-inch, heavy,
nonstick frying pan. Once the oil is hot, add half of the tofu
sticks and cook until golden brown on all sides, turning over
halfway through, about 9 minutes. Transfer to a plate, and
repeat with the remaining tofu, about another 9 minutes.

7. Add the snow peas, lettuce, carrots, tomatoes, cucumbers,
¼ teaspoon salt, the remaining pepper, and ½ cup of dressing
to a large bowl and toss gently with tongs. (Add the dressing right before serving so the salad stays crisp.) Divide the
salad among four large plates. On top of each serving, arrange
3 pan-fried tofu strips and 2 hard-cooked egg halves. Drizzle
a tablespoon of the dressing on top of each serving, then
sprinkle with about a tablespoon of the chopped peanuts
and serve.

SERVING SUGGESTIONS: To cap off your lunch, serve coconut or lime sorbet with sliced strawberries.

TRY THIS: If you can, wash and spin-dry the lettuce leaves
in advance, so they have time to dry out, chill, and crisp up
in the refrigerator (store in the salad spinner in the fridge
until you're ready to use them). For ease, you can purchase
preshredded carrots, but know they won't taste as fresh.

Spiced Vegetable and Paneer Stew

SERVES 4 TO 6

Saag (spinach) and *mutter* (pea) paneer are two of my favorite Indian dishes. Here, I complement the paneer with lots more vege-tables and use just 2 tablespoons of butter to keep the dish healthier. Paneer is available at international grocers and many gourmet food stores.

2 tablespoons unsalted butter

1 cup finely chopped red onions

1 cup small-dice carrots

1 tablespoon minced peeled fresh ginger

2 teaspoons seeded minced jalapeño

2 teaspoons minced garlic

1½ teaspoons garam masala

⅛ teaspoon turmeric

⅛ teaspoon cayenne pepper

3 cups small-dice starchy potatoes, such as Russet

3 cups small cauliflower florets

5 tablespoons tomato paste

3 cups reduced-sodium vegetable broth

1 cup chopped cored tomatoes

2 tablespoons fresh-squeezed, strained lime juice

1½ teaspoons coarse salt

8 ounces paneer, cut into roughly ⅓-inch dice (scant 2 cups)

2 cups frozen peas, thawed

Finely chopped fresh cilantro leaves

Thinly sliced scallions, white and light green parts only

1. Melt the butter over medium-high heat in a heavy Dutch oven. Once melted, add the onions, carrots, ginger, jalapeño, garlic, garam masala, turmeric, and cayenne, and sauté until the vegetables are slightly softened, about 3 minutes. Add the potatoes and cauliflower and sauté for 4 minutes. Add the tomato paste and sauté for 3 minutes, stirring occasionally. Add the broth, tomatoes, lime juice, and salt; stir well and simmer, covered, for 15 minutes.

2. Add the paneer, cover, and reduce the heat to medium low. Simmer until the potatoes and cauliflower are tender, about 20 minutes. Two minutes before this time has elapsed, stir in the peas. Sprinkle with cilantro and scallions and serve.

SERVING SUGGESTIONS: This Indian stew would be delicious served over basmati rice, with yogurt or raita and mango chutney on the side. For dessert, try mango-yogurt lassis (smoothies).

TRY THIS: Paneer is a soft, mild cheese very common in South Asia. Prepared from milk and an acid (such as lemon juice), it is fresh (not aged) and unsalted. Since it doesn't melt, it's ideal for stews.

Mexican Chopped Salad with Cornbread Croutons

SERVES 4

This family-style entrée salad is full of color and flavor. Warning: The cornbread croutons are incredibly addictive and make a delicious stand-alone snack (that's why this recipe includes a healthy amount!). Zest the lime before you juice it. Pick a chile powder that includes just ground dried chile—no salt. Prepare the dressing right before serving for the most vivid green color, and make sure the lettuce is cold and dry, for maximum crispness.

4 cups 1-inch cubes corn muffins or corn cakes

2 tablespoons extra-virgin olive oil

½ teaspoon ground cumin

½ teaspoon ancho chile powder

1 garlic clove

½ cup mayonnaise

½ cup fresh cilantro leaves

Heaping packed ¼ cup coarsely chopped fresh chives

¼ cup plus 1½ teaspoons fresh-squeezed, strained lime juice, divided

2 tablespoons vegetable oil

1 tablespoon honey

¾ teaspoon seeded coarsely chopped jalapeño

1 teaspoon lime zest

1½ teaspoons coarse salt, divided

5 grinds black pepper

continued

1. Heat the oven to 400°F. Pour the cornbread onto a baking sheet with sides. In a small bowl, whisk the olive oil with the cumin and chile powder. Drizzle over the cornbread and mix gently, but well, with your hands. Bake until golden brown and a bit crisp, 12 to 15 minutes.

2. Meanwhile, add the garlic to the bowl of a food processor, and process until finely chopped, about 8 seconds. Add the mayonnaise, cilantro, chives, 3 tablespoons of the lime juice, the vegetable oil, honey, jalapeño, lime zest, ¼ teaspoon salt, and 5 grinds pepper. Process until smooth, about 20 seconds (you should have about ¾ cup).

3. In a medium bowl, toss together the lettuce with ¼ teaspoon salt. Transfer to the center of a large white platter (make a pile). Arrange the cheese cubes in a clump next to the lettuce. In the same bowl, toss together the corn with ⅛ teaspoon salt; transfer to the platter in another pile. In the same bowl, toss together the jìcama with ¼ teaspoon salt and 1½ teaspoons lime juice; transfer to the platter in another pile. In the same bowl, toss together the tomatoes with ¼ teaspoon salt; transfer to the platter in another clump. In the same bowl, toss together the radishes with ⅛ teaspoon salt and transfer to the platter in another pile. Arrange the avocado slices on

continued

4 cups coarsely chopped cored romaine heart leaves, washed and spun dry

½ pound sharp Cheddar or Monterey Jack, cubed

1 packed cup fresh, raw corn kernels

1 cup matchstick slices peeled jìcama

1 cup halved cherry or grape tomatoes

¼ cup plus 2 tablespoons thinly sliced radishes

2 ripe avocados, pitted and sliced

the platter in another pile. Drizzle the remaining tablespoon of the lime juice all over the avocado slices, and sprinkle them evenly with ¼ teaspoon salt. (See the picture of the finished salad on p. 77 for help arranging the ingredients—you don't want any piles that are the same color next to each other.)

4. Serve at the table, with the dressing alongside. Everyone should drizzle 2 to 3 tablespoons of dressing over their portion.

SERVING SUGGESTIONS: For dessert, offer a mango tart or mango sorbet with cinnamon-sugar cookies.

TRY THIS: Make this salad vegan by preparing vegan corn-bread and using vegan mayonnaise, agave nectar instead of honey, and vegan cheese.

Roasted Beet Salad with Toasted Walnuts and Chickpea-Avocado Vinaigrette

SERVES 4

This vegan salad—featuring sweet-tart vinegar-tossed roasted beets, crunchy frisée and walnuts, and a creamy avocado-chickpea dressing— is the ultimate light, healthful lunch. Watch the walnuts when toasting, so they don't burn.

1 pound beets

2 tablespoons sherry vinegar or red-wine vinegar

1 scant teaspoon coarse salt, divided

11 grinds black pepper, divided

¼ cup plus 3 tablespoons extra-virgin olive oil

One 15-ounce can chickpeas (garbanzo beans), rinsed and drained, divided

1 ripe avocado, cut in half, pitted, divided

2 tablespoons fresh-squeezed, strained lemon juice

1 tablespoon chopped shallots

½ teaspoon chopped garlic

¼ teaspoon ground cumin

¼ teaspoon ground coriander

⅛ teaspoon ground cayenne pepper

4 packed cups frisée, cored, washed, spun dry, and torn into bite-sized pieces

1 cup chopped walnuts, lightly toasted

1. Heat the oven to 400°F. Wrap the beets tightly in foil and roast until they are tender but still retain their shape, about 1 hour and 20 minutes. Let cool, then peel, trim the ends, and cut into roughly ¼-inch dice (you should have about 2 cups). Pour into a medium bowl, and toss well with the vinegar, ⅛ teaspoon salt, and 4 grinds pepper. Set aside.

2. Add the oil, 2½ tablespoons chickpeas, the flesh of half of the avocado, the lemon juice, shallots, garlic, cumin, coriander, cayenne, ¼ teaspoon salt, and 4 grinds pepper to a blender or food processor. Purée until smooth, about 40 seconds (you should yield about ⅔ cup thick dressing). Set the dressing aside.

3. Add the frisée, the remaining chickpeas, ¼ plus ⅛ teaspoon salt, and all of the dressing to a medium bowl. Use tongs to toss, coating the frisée with the dressing. Slice the remaining avocado half into 8 slices, line them up, and sprinkle evenly with ⅛ teaspoon salt and 3 grinds pepper.

4. Using tongs, divide the frisée-chickpea mixture among four plates. Place 2 slices of the seasoned avocado on each plate. Sprinkle a quarter of the seasoned beets and a quarter of the toasted nuts on top of each salad, and serve.

SERVING SUGGESTIONS: Serve with warm pita and hummus, and offer baklava or orange sorbet and dates for dessert.

TRY THIS: To toast nuts, place them on a baking sheet and roast in a 325°F oven for 8 to 10 minutes, or just until they start to smell toasted. Remove and let cool before using.

Zucchini Fritters with Fresh Mint and Pecorino

These fritters are light, tender, and packed with flavor. If you prefer, use Parmigiano-Reggiano instead of pecorino. The former, made with cow's milk, is nuttier and sweeter; the latter, made from sheep's milk, is a bit saltier and tangier.

4 packed cups grated zucchini

1½ cups freshly grated pecorino

¼ cup finely chopped fresh flat-leaf parsley leaves

3 tablespoons finely chopped fresh mint leaves

1 tablespoon lemon zest

3 large eggs, well beaten

1 cup unbleached all-purpose flour

1 teaspoon baking powder

¾ teaspoon coarse salt

8 grinds black pepper

About ¼ cup plus 2 tablespoons extra-virgin olive oil, divided

About 2 cups plain Greek yogurt, for serving

1. Spoon the grated zucchini onto a clean kitchen towel and gather up into a bundle. Squeeze well over the sink to remove any excess liquid. Transfer the drained zucchini to a large bowl and stir in the cheese, parsley, mint, lemon zest, and beaten eggs. In a medium bowl, whisk together the flour, baking powder, salt, and pepper. Add to the zucchini mixture, and mix well.

2. Heat ¼ cup oil in a 10-inch, heavy, nonstick sauté pan over medium-high heat. When hot, use an ice cream scoop to dollop roughly 5 mounds of batter onto the hot oil. Pan-fry, pressing down a bit to flatten, until the first side is golden brown, 3 to 4 minutes. Use a spatula to carefully flip and cook the other side until it is also golden brown, about another 3 minutes. Transfer to a paper towel–lined baking sheet. Repeat with the remaining batter, using the remaining 2 tablespoons of oil when the pan goes dry. Serve the fritters immediately with Greek yogurt.

SERVING SUGGESTIONS: Serve these Italian-inspired, easy-to-prepare fritters alongside a salad of watermelon, tomato, cucumber, olives, and feta. For dessert, offer vanilla gelato sprinkled with freshly grated lemon zest.

Creamy Mexican Carrot Soup with Black Bean Toasts

SERVES 6 (WITH SOME EXTRA SOUP)

Dip the toasts (slathered with bean dip) into the spiced, velvety soup on cold days. If reheating, feel free to thin it out with vegetable broth; just adjust the seasoning with more salt, if necessary. To make the soup vegan, either omit the sour cream or use a dairy-free yogurt and substitute agave nectar or maple syrup for the honey.

FOR THE SOUP

2 tablespoons vegetable oil

2 cups coarsely chopped finely chopped red onions

¼ plus ⅛ teaspoon ground cumin

¼ plus ⅛ teaspoon ancho chili powder

8 cups coarsely chopped carrots

7 cups reduced-sodium vegetable broth

½ cup sour cream

¼ cup plus 3 tablespoons fresh-squeezed, strained lime juice

¼ cup plus 1 tablespoon honey

¼ cup plus 1 tablespoon fresh, whole cilantro leaves

1 tablespoons liquid from a can of chipotle chiles en adobo, divided

2½ teaspoons coarse salt

FOR THE BLACK BEAN TOASTS

Three ½-inch-thick slices country bread

½ cup vegetable oil, divided

¾ teaspoons coarse salt, divided

continued

MAKE THE SOUP

1. Heat the oven to 400°F. Heat the oil in a large, heavy Dutch oven over medium-high heat. When hot, add the onions, the cumin, and chili powder and sauté until softened, about 6 minutes. Add the carrots and sauté, stirring occasionally with a wooden spoon, for another 5 minutes. Add the broth and bring to a boil over high heat. Cook until the carrots are very tender when pierced with a sharp knife, 30 to 35 minutes. Turn off the heat.

2. Use an immersion blender to carefully purée until no chunks remain, about 3 minutes (be vigilant to make sure all of the chunks are gone). If you don't have an immersion or stick blender, purée in batches in a blender, not filling the blender jar more than halfway and holding down the lid with a kitchen towel.

3. Add the sour cream, lime juice, honey, the whole cilantro leaves, chipotle liquid, and salt; purée with the immersion blender to mix well. (You will have about 13 cups of soup.)

MAKE THE BLACK BEAN TOASTS

1. Place the bread on a baking sheet with sides. Brush evenly with ¼ cup oil. Sprinkle evenly with a total of a scant ¼ teaspoon salt. Bake until crisp and slightly golden brown, about 15 minutes.

continued

One 15-ounce can black beans, rinsed and drained

¼ cup fresh, whole cilantro leaves, plus another ¼ cup finely chopped fresh cilantro leaves, for serving

2 tablespoons finely chopped red onions

2 tablespoons fresh-squeezed, strained lime juice

1½ teaspoons liquid from a can of chipotle chiles en adobo

¼ teaspoon ground cumin

¼ teaspoon ancho chili powder

2. While the bread bakes, in a food processor (a miniature model will work fine here), combine the rinsed and drained beans, the remaining ¼ cup oil, ¼ cup fresh whole cilantro leaves, onions, lime juice, chipotle liquid, the remaining ½ teaspoon salt, cumin, and chili powder. Purée until smooth, 1 to 2 minutes. (You'll have 1 cup of spread.)

3. Ladle 2 cups of soup into each of six large serving bowls. Spread about 2½ tablespoons of the bean mixture onto each slice of bread; cut each slice into quarters and sprinkle with chopped fresh cilantro. Serve two quarters with each portion of soup.

SERVING SUGGESTIONS: Accompany the soup with an avocado, radish, and romaine salad with lime dressing, and offer Mexican wedding cookies for dessert.

TRY THIS: Give this entrée an Indian spin by substituting garam masala for the cumin and chili powder. Serve with warm naan brushed with butter or trans-fat-free margarine and sprinkled with finely chopped fresh mint leaves. Omit the black bean toasts.

Cuban Black Bean Stew with Sweet Plantains

SERVES 4

If you've never had sweet plantains, you are in for a treat. Select plantains (found near the bananas in the market) that are very ripe—with lots of dark spots—but not mushy or falling apart. Thanks to the tomato paste, chipotle liquid, soy sauce, beer, and coconut milk, this stew is extremely flavorful—and satisfying. Avowed carnivores won't miss the pork typically present in such a dish. Make this vegan by using a butter substitute and a vegan yogurt.

2 tablespoons unsalted butter or vegetable oil

1 cup finely chopped onions

1 cup finely chopped red bell peppers, seeds and membranes removed

1 tablespoon minced garlic

1 teaspoon seeded finely chopped jalapeño

¼ teaspoon ground cumin

2 tablespoons tomato paste

1½ teaspoons sauce from a can of chipotle chiles en adobo

⅓ cup mild lager beer

Two 13.4-ounce cans black beans, rinsed and drained

1 cup light coconut milk

½ cup reduced-sodium vegetable broth

3 tablespoons fresh-squeezed, strained lime juice

2 tablespoons reduced-sodium tamari soy sauce

½ teaspoon coarse salt, divided

continued

1. Melt the butter in a heavy, medium-sized saucepot over medium-high heat. Once melted, add the onions, bell peppers, garlic, jalapeño, and cumin, and sauté until softened, about 4 minutes. Stir in the tomato paste and chipotle liquid and cook, stirring occasionally, for 1 minute. Carefully add the beer and simmer for 1 minute. Add the beans, coconut milk, broth, lime juice, soy sauce, and ¼ teaspoon salt, and simmer until slightly thickened and the flavors meld, about 12 minutes. Turn off the heat and stir in the fresh parsley or cilantro leaves. (You will have about 1 quart soup.)

2. Meanwhile, heat the oil in a 12-inch, heavy, nonstick frying pan over medium-high heat. When hot but not smoking, carefully add half of the plantain slices and cook the first side until golden brown, about 4 minutes, pressing down a bit with a spatula to slightly flatten. Very carefully flip the slices over and cook the other side until they are similarly golden brown, about another 3 minutes. Transfer to a paper towel–lined baking sheet. Carefully add the remaining plantain slices, reduce the heat to medium (since the pan will now be very hot), and cook until both sides are golden brown, about 5 minutes total. Transfer to the baking sheet. Press the plantain slices with another paper towel to drain off any excess oil. Line up the slices and sprinkle evenly with the remaining ¼ teaspoon salt.

continued

¼ cup finely chopped fresh flat-leaf parsley or cilantro leaves

⅓ cup vegetable oil

2 very ripe plantains, peeled and sliced on the bias ⅓ inch thick

Sour cream or plain dairy-free yogurt, for garnish (optional)

3. Ladle 1 cup of stew into each of four serving bowls. If desired, spoon a dollop of sour cream or yogurt on top of the stew. Serve a quarter of the plantain slices with each bowl of stew.

SERVING SUGGESTIONS: Begin your meal with a salad of avocado slices, hearts of palm, and fresh mango, and end with flan or coconut sorbet.

TRY THIS: To easily remove the peel from the plantain, slice off both ends and then make a very shallow slit down the entire side, following its natural curves.

Miso Soup with Fresh Udon Noodles and Root Vegetables

SERVES 4

Lots of miso paste, plus soy sauce and mirin (sweet Japanese rice wine) add oomph to this fish-free soup (traditional miso soup is flavored with bonito, or tuna, flakes). For a more mild broth, begin with just ⅓ cup of miso (and add another ⅓ cup later if desired). Look for fresh udon noodles in the refrigerated section (with the tofu) at most markets, while kombu and mirin can be found in the Asian section.

One 9-ounce package fresh (refrigerated) udon noodles

One 2-inch knob fresh ginger root, peeled and cut into 4 pieces

8 cups reduced-sodium vegetable broth

Two 6-inch-long pieces dried kombu (kelp)

¼ cup plus 2 tablespoons reduced-sodium soy sauce

¼ cup plus 2 tablespoons mirin

1 cup very thinly sliced carrots

1 cup very thinly sliced peeled yams

½ cup very thinly sliced peeled parsnips

2 cups snow peas, string removed

⅔ cup brown rice miso paste

1 pound extra-firm plain tofu, cubed

⅓ cup thinly sliced scallions, white and light green parts only

1. Fill a large pot two-thirds full of water, cover, and bring to a boil. Once the water is boiling, add the noodles and stir well. Cook, stirring occasionally, following the package instructions (they should take 2 or 3 minutes). Drain and set aside.

2. Meanwhile, wrap the ginger in a small piece of cheesecloth, form into a bundle, and secure closed with kitchen twine. In a large, heavy Dutch oven, bring the broth, kombu, ginger sack, soy sauce, and mirin to a boil over medium-high heat. Once the broth comes to a boil, reduce the heat to medium and add the carrots, yams, and parsnips. Simmer until the vegetables are tender, about 8 minutes. Stir in the snow peas and simmer until cooked, 1 to 2 minutes.

3. While the snow peas cook, whisk together the miso paste and 1 cup of the hot broth in a small bowl until fairly smooth. Add back to the pot of broth and stir in the cooked noodles, tofu, and scallions; simmer for 1 minute (do not boil). Remove and discard the kombu pieces and ginger sack. Use a ladle and tongs to transfer the soup to bowls and serve.

SERVING SUGGESTIONS: Serve this light vegan meal with a green salad dressed with a ginger vinaigrette. Offer green tea ice cream with almond cookies for dessert.

TRY THIS: Ginger is easiest to peel using a metal tablespoon. Simply scrape it along the skin of the piece of ginger, working around the knobs and gnarly parts.

Cold Pan-Asian Noodle Salad with Tomatoes, Tofu, and Daikon

SERVES 4 TO 6

If you like your food extra-spicy, use more jalapeño or a hotter chile pepper. And if you can't find daikon, just substitute more carrot or bell pepper. ❡ Feel free to make this salad with other Asian noodles, such as cellophane. Just follow the package directions for preparing them.

About 9 ounces snap peas (2 cups)

One 8-ounce package Asian brown rice noodles

¼ cup plus 2 tablespoons peanut oil

¼ cup reduced-sodium soy sauce

3 tablespoons unseasoned rice vinegar

2 tablespoons fresh-squeezed, strained lime juice

2 tablespoons maple syrup

1½ teaspoons minced shallots

1 teaspoon seeded minced jalapeño

½ teaspoon minced peeled fresh ginger

¼ teaspoon minced garlic

⅛ teaspoon Sriracha hot sauce

1 cup grape tomatoes, halved

1 cup shredded carrots

1 cup matchstick slices red bell peppers

1 cup matchstick slices peeled daikon

continued

1. Fill a medium-sized pot with about 2 inches of water and a steamer basket, cover, and bring to a boil over high heat. Once boiling, place the snap peas in the steamer basket, cover, and steam until crisp-tender and still bright green, about 6 minutes. Immediately transfer to a bowl of salted ice water, swish around for a minute, and then drain. Place the drained snap peas in a large bowl.

2. Fill a large pot two-thirds full of salted water, cover, and bring to a boil over high heat. When the water comes to a boil, remove the pot from the heat. Add the noodles and stir well. Let sit until the noodles are tender, about 5 minutes. Pour into a colander set in the sink to drain, and then rinse with very cold water until chilled.

3. In a medium bowl, make the dressing: Whisk together the peanut oil, soy sauce, rice vinegar, lime juice, maple syrup, shallots, jalapeño, ginger, garlic, and Sriracha (you should yield about 1 cup).

4. Add the noodles, grape tomatoes, carrots, red peppers, daikon, mint, cilantro, red onions, scallions, and salt to the bowl of snap peas. Add about three-quarters of the dressing and toss well with tongs. Add the tofu and the remaining dressing and toss again, very gently but thoroughly (so as not to break up the tofu). Serve.

continued

¼ cup plus 3 tablespoons finely chopped fresh mint leaves

¼ cup plus 3 tablespoons finely chopped fresh cilantro leaves

½ cup thinly sliced halved red onions

¼ cup sliced scallions, white and light green parts only

1½ teaspoons coarse salt

One 14-ounce package extra-firm tofu, diced

SERVING SUGGESTIONS: This refreshing, vegan pan-Asian salad is ideal paired with steamed edamame. Serve mochi or green tea ice cream floats (with coconut milk ice cream) for dessert.

TRY THIS: Daikon root, an East Asian radish, looks like a large, fat, white carrot. In taste and texture, it's similar to a radish: crisp, juicy, and slightly bitter and peppery. Try it pickled, sautéed, boiled in soups, and sliced raw in salads.

Tartines of Grilled Bread with Whipped Herbed Goat Cheese and Balsamic Shiitakes

SERVES 4

This simple dish is a fun, sophisticated variation on grilled cheese. Creamy, herb-flecked goat cheese spread contrasts with earthy sautéed mushrooms that are slightly sweet from balsamic vinegar and honey; chopped fresh parsley adds color and vibrancy. The large slices of bread make these fork-and-knife open-face sandwiches substantial.

8 ounces fresh goat cheese

½ cup 2% milk

2 tablespoons coarsely chopped fresh chives

1 tablespoon fresh thyme leaves

¾ teaspoon coarse salt, divided

18 grinds black pepper, divided

¼ cup plus 3 tablespoons extra-virgin olive oil, divided

½ cup minced shallots (from 8 medium shallots)

12 ounces shiitake mushrooms, stems removed and caps cut into roughly ½-inch pieces

1 teaspoon minced fresh rosemary sprigs

¼ cup balsamic vinegar

2 tablespoons sherry vinegar or red-wine vinegar

2 teaspoons honey

4 large 1-inch-thick slices high-quality country bread, such as *pain de campagne*

¼ cup coarsely chopped fresh flat-leaf parsley leaves

1. Add the goat cheese, milk, chives, thyme, ¼ teaspoon salt, and 8 grinds pepper to a food processor. Purée until smooth, about 30 seconds (you should have about 1¼ cups). Set aside.

2. Add 2 tablespoons of the oil to a 10-inch, heavy, nonstick sauté pan over medium-high heat. When hot, add the shallots and sauté until softened and aromatic, about 3 minutes. Add the mushrooms, rosemary, ¼ teaspoon salt, and 10 grinds pepper. Sauté until all of the liquid from the mushrooms has evaporated, about 6 minutes. In a small bowl, mix together the balsamic and sherry vinegars and the honey. Add to the mushrooms and continue simmering and stirring until the liquid evaporates, about another 5 minutes.

3. While the mushrooms cook, brush both sides of the bread slices with ¼ cup oil. Sprinkle both sides evenly with the remaining ¼ teaspoon salt. Brush a 10-inch, heavy, nonstick grill pan with the remaining 1 tablespoon oil. Heat over medium high. When hot, add the bread slices, pressing them down flat. Grill until grill marks appear and the bread crisps up, 3 to 5 minutes per side, turning over halfway through.

4. Top each bread slice with about 2 tablespoons of the goat cheese mixture (spread to cover with a small rubber spatula), then about 5 tablespoons of the mushroom mixture, and then about 1 tablespoon of the chopped parsley. Serve immediately.

SERVING SUGGESTIONS: Serve with a beet, frisée, and walnut salad, with chocolate-dipped dried apricots for dessert.

Greek Salad with Roasted Spiced Chickpeas and Watermelon

One of my favorite salads is watermelon with feta cheese, arugula, olive oil, black pepper, and a bit of sea salt. I love the interplay between the sweet melon, salty cheese, and spicy arugula. I build on that combination here, adding the chickpeas to make this twist on Greek salad more substantial and using butter lettuce for crunch and sweetness. If you can't find sweet ripe (but not over-ripe) watermelon, use pomegranate seeds. Before beginning, zest the lemon and then squeeze the juice. Leave the dressing out at room temperature so it's pourable.

FOR THE DRESSING

- ¼ cup plus 2 tablespoons extra-virgin olive oil
- 2 tablespoons fresh-squeezed, strained lemon juice
- 2 tablespoons red-wine vinegar
- 1½ teaspoons honey
- 1½ teaspoons minced fresh oregano leaves
- 1 teaspoon lemon zest
- ½ teaspoon coarse salt
- 3 grinds black pepper

FOR THE SALAD

- One 15-ounce can chickpeas, rinsed and drained
- 2 tablespoons extra-virgin olive oil; more for the pan
- 2 teaspoons fresh-squeezed, strained lemon juice
- 1 teaspoon minced fresh oregano leaves
- ¾ teaspoon coarse salt, divided

1. In a small bowl, whisk together all of the dressing ingredients and set aside.

2. Heat the oven to 400°F. Line a baking sheet with foil and lightly grease with oil or cooking spray. In a medium bowl, toss together the chickpeas, oil, lemon juice, oregano, ½ teaspoon salt, the thyme, paprika, cumin, cayenne, and 3 grinds black pepper. Mix well and then spread on the prepared baking sheet. Roast until the chickpeas are golden brown and a bit crisp, about 35 minutes. Set aside to cool to room temperature.

3. In a large salad bowl, toss together all of the dressing with the cooled chickpeas, the cucumbers, tomatoes, onions, lettuce, dill, remaining ¼ teaspoon salt, and remaining 3 grinds pepper. Add the watermelon, olives, and feta, and toss again very gently. Serve immediately.

½ teaspoon minced fresh
   thyme leaves

¼ teaspoon paprika

⅛ teaspoon ground cumin

1/16 teaspoon ground cayenne

6 grinds black pepper, divided

2 cups ⅓-inch dice English
   cucumbers

2 cups whole cherry tomatoes

1 cup ⅓-inch dice red onions,
   soaked in cold water for
   30 minutes and drained

5 ounces butter lettuce leaves,
   washed and spun dry

Scant ½ cup finely chopped
   fresh dill

Scant 2 cups ⅓-inch dice
   seedless watermelon flesh

¾ cup pitted kalamata olives

5 ounces crumbled feta cheese

SERVING SUGGESTION: This salad needs no accompaniment other than perhaps some warm pita bread. Serve baklava for dessert.

TRY THIS: I must confess: I often purchase my watermelon already halved or quartered so I can see the flesh. I choose fruit that is bright red (so it will have plenty of sweet flavor) but still firm, without darker or sunken-in sections. Those softer parts are over-ripe and tend to have an off-taste.

Tomato-Mozzarella Sandwiches with Black Olive Tapenade

SERVES 4

These classic Italian sandwiches are delicious cold (if you're in a rush) or hot (if you want a golden, crispy exterior and molten cheese). If you have a panini press, use it; you can also try pressing down on the sandwiches with foil-wrapped bricks to simulate that effect. ¶ Since the sandwiches are so simple, be sure to purchase high-quality bread, cheese, tomatoes, and basil, and don't skip the step of draining the fillings. Store your tomatoes at room temperature to maintain their flavor and texture. To make these sandwiches vegan, simply substitute soy cheese or even plain extra-firm tofu (drained very well between several layers of kitchen towels). ¶ The tapenade recipe yields more than you'll need for these sandwiches; the remainder will last for up to a week. Feel free to use a mix of darker olives (such as Kalamata or niçoise). Or, make a green tapenade by swapping in green olives and white or golden balsamic vinegar.

4 ripe, juicy tomatoes, each cored and thinly sliced

1 pound fresh mozzarella, at room temperature, thinly sliced

About 24 fresh basil leaves, rinsed

About ½ teaspoon coarse salt

About 20 grinds black pepper

¾ cup Black Olive Tapenade (recipe follows)

One 1-pound loaf ciabatta bread, sliced in half horizontally, then again four times vertically

About ¼ cup olive oil

1. Lay the tomato slices on a paper towel and dab with a second paper towel. Do the same with the sliced cheese and basil. Sprinkle the tomatoes evenly with the salt and pepper.

2. Spread 1 tablespoon tapenade onto each of 4 slices of bread and 2 tablespoons tapenade on each of the remaining 4 slices of bread (for a total of ¾ cup tapenade). Divide the seasoned tomatoes, then the cheese, and then the basil among the slices of bread with 2 tablespoons tapenade. Top with the remaining 4 bread slices, with the tapenade sides facing down (don't overload the sandwiches too much, as you want them to stay together in the pan).

3. Brush the insides of two medium-sized, heavy, nonstick grill pans with the oil, and heat over medium. When hot, add 2 sandwiches per pan, and cook until the first side becomes golden brown and crisp, about 5 minutes. Very carefully turn the sandwiches over, reduce the heat to low, cover completely, and cook until the sides facing down become golden brown and crisp, the cheese melts, and the sandwiches are warm, about another 5 minutes. If desired, cut each sandwich in half and serve with additional tapenade for dipping.

SERVING SUGGESTIONS: For dessert, use a melon baller to prepare various types of melon (such as honeydew, watermelon, and cantaloupe), and toss with lime syrup; chill and serve cold.

TRY THIS: If you can't find pitted olives, use the flat side of your chef's knife to crush the olives, then pick out the pits.

BLACK OLIVE TAPENADE

YIELDS 2 CUPS

2 large garlic cloves

2 cups pitted black olives

One 2.4-ounce jar capers, rinsed and drained

1 packed teaspoon lemon zest

1 heaping tablespoon fresh oregano leaves

¼ cup plus 1 tablespoon balsamic vinegar

1 tablespoon red-wine vinegar

1 teaspoon granulated sugar

5 grinds black pepper

⅛ teaspoon Aleppo pepper or crushed red pepper flakes

½ cup extra-virgin olive oil

Add the garlic to the bowl of a food processor and process until finely chopped, about 5 seconds. Add all of the remaining ingredients except for the oil, and purée until well mixed and smooth, about 10 seconds. Add the oil and purée until very smooth, about another 10 seconds.

Quinoa-Polenta Cakes with Roasted Red Pepper Sauce and White Bean Purée

SERVES 4; MAKES ABOUT 19 CAKES, ABOUT 1¼ CUPS SAUCE, AND 1½ CUPS PURÉE

This healthful, satisfying dish (vegan if you use a soy cheese) was inspired by one of my favorite entrées at Le Pain Quotidien. If the quinoa is not prerinsed, be sure to rinse it thoroughly to remove the grain's bitter taste. Roasting your own bell peppers will lend your sauce the best flavor; however, in a pinch, you can go with jarred.

FOR THE ROASTED RED PEPPER SAUCE

3 small garlic cloves

1 cup chopped roasted red peppers (see p. 7)

¼ cup extra-virgin olive oil

2 tablespoons tomato paste

1 tablespoon honey

1 teaspoon fresh oregano leaves

½ teaspoon coarse salt

3 grinds black pepper

FOR THE WHITE BEAN PURÉE

1 small garlic clove

One 15-ounce can white beans, rinsed and drained

¼ cup plus 2 tablespoons extra-virgin olive oil

3 tablespoons fresh-squeezed, strained lemon juice

1 tablespoon white balsamic vinegar

¾ teaspoon coarse salt

½ teaspoon chopped fresh rosemary sprigs

continued

MAKE THE PEPPER SAUCE

In a mini food processor, pulse the garlic until minced, about 10 seconds. Add the remaining ingredients, and purée until smooth, about 20 seconds.

MAKE THE WHITE BEAN PURÉE

Clean out the mini food processor bowl, then add the garlic and pulse until minced, about 10 seconds. Add the remaining ingredients, and purée until smooth, 30 to 40 seconds.

MAKE THE CAKES

1. Bring 4 cups of the broth, plus half of the salt and all of the pepper to a boil in a deep, heavy medium saucepan over high heat. Once the broth has come to a boil, gradually stir in the polenta and reduce the heat to medium low. Cook, stirring vigorously and frequently, until the polenta is tender and the separate grains are no longer visible, about 23 minutes (expect a thin layer of the polenta to stick to the bottom of the pan). Transfer to a large bowl.

2. Meanwhile, bring the remaining 2 cups broth to a boil in a heavy medium saucepan over high heat. Once the broth is boiling, stir in the quinoa. Making sure the broth is still boiling, cover the pan, and reduce the heat to medium low.

continued

FOR THE QUINOA-POLENTA CAKES

6 cups low-sodium vegetable broth, divided

2 teaspoons coarse salt, divided

8 grinds black pepper

1 cup polenta (or corn grits)

1 cup prewashed quinoa

1 cup grated Parmigiano-Reggiano

1 cup grated carrots

1 cup grated zucchini, squeezed well to drain of excess water

½ cup unbleached all-purpose flour

¼ cup finely chopped fresh flat-leaf parsley leaves

About ½ cup extra-virgin olive oil, for cooking the cakes

Simmer the quinoa until it is cooked through (the white squiggles in the center of each grain will be visible, and each grain will be soft and larger in size) and all of the liquid has evaporated, about 15 minutes. Transfer the cooked quinoa, cheese, carrots, squeezed zucchini, flour, parsley, and the remaining 1 teaspoon salt to the large bowl with the cooked polenta. Stir very well.

3. Heat 3 tablespoons of the oil in a 10-inch, heavy, nonstick sauté pan over medium-high heat. When the oil is hot, form seven 2-inch oval patties of the quinoa-vegetable mixture, and add to the oil. Cook until the first side is golden brown and a bit crispy, about 3 minutes. Using a nonstick spatula, gently flip the cakes and cook until the second side is similarly golden brown and a bit crispy, about another 3 minutes. Transfer to a paper towel–lined baking sheet to degrease. Repeat with the remaining oil and patties, never letting the pan go dry. You should end up with about 19 cakes.

ASSEMBLE THE DISH AND SERVE

For each serving, spoon about 3 tablespoons of the white bean purée onto the center of a plate. Place 3 or 4 cakes on top. Drizzle about 3 tablespoons of the red pepper sauce over the top. Serve.

SERVING SUGGESTIONS: A full meal on their own, the cakes would be delicious followed by a plum tart or peach ice cream.

TRY THIS: Fantastic reheated (warm the oven to 300°F and heat, uncovered, on a baking sheet), these cakes would be ideal for a party; just form smaller versions and serve them as appetizers.

Phyllo Dough Napoleons with Ricotta, Summer Vegetables, and Pesto

SERVES 4

This showstopping dish is filling (from the ricotta and crispy phyllo) yet light (from the vibrant summer vegetables). Feel free to vary the vegetables; for instance, pattypan squash or halved baby tomatoes would be delicious in place of the zucchini and corn. Phyllo dough—found in the freezer section at the grocery store—usually comes in 1-pound boxes. Be sure to rinse the leek well to remove any dirt (see Try This on p. 100).

8 sheets phyllo dough

8 tablespoons (1 stick) unsalted butter, 6 tablespoons melted, divided

2 cups thinly sliced leeks

1 cup small-dice red bell peppers

2 small garlic cloves plus 2 teaspoons finely chopped garlic, divided

1½ cups small-dice zucchini

1 cup raw corn kernels

About 1¾ teaspoons coarse salt, divided

1 packed cup fresh basil leaves

¼ cup pine nuts

½ cup extra-virgin olive oil

¼ cup packed grated Parmigiano-Reggiano

1 pint part-skim ricotta

¼ cup minced fresh chives

1 teaspoon lemon zest

BAKE THE PHYLLO DOUGH

1. Heat the oven to 350°F. Cut two sheets of parchment paper to fit the inside of a baking sheet with sides. Spray the inside of the baking sheet with cooking spray, and then lay down one sheet of parchment (so it sticks). Spray the parchment with cooking spray. Arrange the sheets of phyllo dough on a clean surface and cover with a large piece of plastic wrap and a very damp, clean kitchen towel. Carefully place 1 sheet of phyllo on top of the greased parchment and brush with some of the melted butter, beginning with the edges (leave the remaining sheets of phyllo covered with the plastic wrap and damp towel). Immediately top with another sheet of phyllo, and brush with more butter. Repeat until you have used all 8 sheets of phyllo, brushing the last layer with butter.

2. With a very sharp knife, score 8 evenly sized squares, cutting all the way through. Brush the other piece of parchment paper with butter. Place this parchment paper, butter side down, on top of the phyllo. Cover with another baking sheet, and transfer to the oven. Bake until golden brown and crisp, about 25 minutes. Remove from the oven and let cool.

MAKE THE VEGETABLE FILLING

Meanwhile, heat the remaining 2 tablespoons butter in a 10-inch heavy sauté pan over medium heat. Once melted, add the leeks,

continued

bell peppers, and 2 teaspoons finely chopped garlic, and sauté until tender, about 4 minutes. Stir in the zucchini and sauté for 3 minutes. Add the corn and ¾ teaspoon salt; stir well and sauté until all of the vegetables are tender, about another 3 minutes. Set aside off of the heat.

PREPARE THE PESTO AND SEASONED RICOTTA FILLING

Add the 2 garlic cloves to the food processor and pulse until minced, about 10 seconds. Add the basil leaves, pine nuts, and ½ teaspoon salt, and purée until finely minced, scraping down the sides of the bowl with a rubber spatula, about 10 seconds. Add the oil and purée until very smooth, about 15 seconds. Stir in the Parmigiano-Reggiano and cover the pesto with a piece of plastic wrap (to preserve its color). (You should have about ¾ cup pesto.) Set aside. In a small bowl, mix together the ricotta, chives, lemon zest, and remaining ½ teaspoon salt. Set aside.

ASSEMBLE THE NAPOLEONS

Place 1 phyllo square on a serving dish. Top with up to one-quarter of the ricotta mixture, then up to one-quarter of the vegetable mixture, letting it sprawl across the plate. Top with one-quarter of the pesto, and then a second phyllo square, arranging it on an angle from the first square. Repeat with the other three servings, and serve.

SERVING SUGGESTIONS: For dessert, serve poached peaches or apricots.

TRY THIS: Leeks are notoriously dirty and must be well rinsed. The best way to do this is to slice what you need and then rinse in a bowl of cold water. Swish the sliced leeks well, and then drain. Fill the bowl with more water, swish again, and then remove the leeks, leaving the dirty water and grit behind.

Leek and Mushroom Quiche

SERVES 6 TO 8

To expedite making this company-worthy quiche, use a store-bought pie or tart shell instead of making one from scratch.

1½ cups plus 1 tablespoon unbleached all-purpose flour, divided

1¼ teaspoons coarse salt, divided

½ teaspoon granulated sugar

8 tablespoons (1 stick) unsalted butter, chilled and cubed, plus another 4 tablespoons (½ stick), divided

3 large eggs plus 1 large egg white, divided

1 tablespoon plus 1 teaspoon cold water (or enough to make the dough form a ball)

10 ounces cremini mushrooms, sliced ¼ inch thick

1 packed cup thinly sliced leeks

1½ teaspoons minced garlic

1 tablespoon finely chopped fresh flat-leaf parsley leaves

¾ cup heavy cream

1 teaspoon Dijon mustard

Zest of 1 lemon

5 grinds black pepper

1 cup grated Gruyère

1. In a medium-sized bowl, whisk together 1½ cups flour, ¾ teaspoon salt, and the sugar until thoroughly mixed. Add the cubed stick of butter and use your fingers to crumble together the mixture until it resembles the consistency of coarse meal. In a small bowl, whisk together one of the eggs with the cold water. Add to the flour mixture and use your hands to massage together until the dough holds together in a ball (if it does not, add another teaspoon of cold water). Immediately wrap the dough in plastic and then flatten into a disk. Chill the dough for at least 30 minutes.

2. Melt 1 tablespoon of the remaining butter, and brush it on the entire inside of a 9- or 9½-inch fluted tart pan with a removable bottom. Sprinkle the remaining 1 tablespoon flour onto a large clean work surface. Remove the dough from the plastic wrap and place it on this surface. Using a rolling pin (with a bench scraper to help you), roll the dough into a circle roughly 12 inches in diameter. Rotate it a couple of times to make sure that it doesn't stick and use a bit more flour if needed. Be sure to work quickly with the dough to keep it cold. Transfer the dough circle to the tart pan. Press it into the bottom and sides of the pan, removing any excess dough (which you can use to patch up any holes). Cover and chill for at least 30 minutes. Heat the oven to 400°F.

3. Meanwhile, heat 2 tablespoons of the remaining butter in a 10-inch, heavy sauté pan over medium-high heat. As soon as the butter has melted, add the mushrooms, leeks, garlic, and ¼ teaspoon of the remaining salt, and sauté until the vegetables are tender and all of the liquid has evaporated from the pan, about 10 minutes. Let cool slightly, then stir in the parsley. In a medium bowl, whisk together 2 of the eggs, the cream, mustard, zest, black pepper, and the remaining ¼ teaspoon salt until smooth.

4. Place the tart shell on a baking sheet. Melt the remaining 1 tablespoon butter and brush on a piece of aluminum foil large enough to cover the shell. Press this foil, butter side down, onto the dough, then top with dried beans or pie weights. Bake for 20 minutes, remove the shell from the oven, and remove the foil and weights. Use a fork to poke about 15 holes all over the bottom of the tart shell, then return it to the oven and bake until very lightly golden, about another 10 minutes.

5. Lightly beat the egg white and brush it on the baked tart shell; let cool for about 10 minutes. Reduce the oven temperature to 350°F.

6. Evenly scatter the vegetable mixture over the bottom of the tart shell (the vegetable mixture should be at room temperature or colder when added). Top with the custard mixture and then the Gruyère. Bake until the inside is set (doesn't jiggle) and the cheese has completely melted, about 30 minutes. Let cool for about 10 minutes and then serve hot (or chill and serve cold or at room temperature).

SERVING SUGGESTIONS: A green salad with a mustard vinaigrette would pair nicely with this quiche. Since it's fairly rich, opt for a fresh, light dessert, such as ripe berries sprinkled with brown sugar and topped with Greek yogurt.

TRY THIS: Weighing down the pie crust as it bakes with pie weights (which are usually small ceramic balls) or dried beans helps keep it flat and even (without air bubbles forming). If you don't have either, no worries: Your quiche might not look as professional, but it will still taste delicious.

CB&J with Cashew Butter and Apricot Preserves

SERVES 4

This new take on PB&J just might be the best such sandwich you've ever had! Make sure to use salted butter, fresh bread, and high-quality preserves. To make these sandwiches vegan, go with a salted, trans-fat-free margarine spread and a rich vegan bread.

Eight ½-inch-thick slices brioche or challah

¾ cup cashew butter, at room temperature

½ cup high-quality apricot preserves

4 tablespoons (½ stick) salted butter

1. Spread 4 bread slices with cashew butter and the remaining 4 with apricot preserves. Then put the bread pieces together, nut butter and preserves facing in, to form sandwiches (make sure no preserves oozes out of the sandwiches).

2. Heat 2 tablespoons of the butter in a 10-inch, heavy nonstick sauté pan over medium heat. Once melted, add 2 sandwiches and cook the first side until golden brown, 2 to 3 minutes. Flip and cook the remaining side, about another 2 minutes (watch carefully, since any preserves that hits the pan can burn). Transfer the sandwiches to a platter. If the pan does not include any burnt bits, add the remaining butter and let it melt. Once it does, cook the remaining 2 sandwiches. If the pan does include burnt bits, turn off the heat; carefully clean out the pan and add the remaining butter; reheat over medium until the butter melts.

3. Cut each sandwich in half and serve immediately.

SERVING SUGGESTION: Serve these sandwiches for brunch alongside eggs, fruit salad, and cappuccino. For an elegant touch, slice into triangle quarters and sprinkle with powdered sugar. For lunch, try them alongside salt and vinegar potato chips and a simple lemon vinaigrette–dressed salad of carrots, apples, and fennel.

Pea *Jibn* with Mediterranean Harvest Salad

SERVES 4

My father's parents hailed from Syria, so I grew up eating a version of this Mideastern pea dish (coin it "peas with eggs and cheese" for less adventurous eaters). Picture a crust-less quiche, but lighter (there's no cream). It is embarrassingly simple and inexpensive to prepare, and just might become one of your weeknight standbys. To vary it, you can swap in other vegetables, such as frozen and thawed bell peppers or spinach (make sure to drain the latter). The accompanying salad, which adds color and freshness to the plate, features the bounty of a typical Mideastern harvest: dates, pomegranates, cucumbers, and tomatoes. ❡ Try to wash and spin-dry the frisée ahead of time; cover with a paper towel and refrigerate for an hour or two to let it crisp up. You'll have ¼ cup of dressing; offer it at the table, in case any diners would like more (they might—it's that good!).

FOR THE PEA *JIBN*

8 large eggs

2 cups shredded Monterey Jack (7 to 8 ounces)

One 10-ounce package frozen baby peas, thawed

¾ teaspoon coarse salt

½ teaspoon ground coriander

5 grinds black pepper

⅛ teaspoon Aleppo pepper or crushed red pepper flakes

continued

MAKE THE PEA *JIBN*

1. Heat the oven to 350°F. Grease an 8 x 8-inch casserole dish with cooking spray. Add the eggs and whisk well. Stir in the cheese, peas, salt, coriander, black pepper, and Aleppo pepper; whisk well.

2. Bake on the upper rack of the oven until the eggs are completely set (poke the center of the dish to check) and golden brown on top, about 50 minutes.

continued

FOR THE MEDITERRANEAN
HARVEST SALAD

¼ cup white-wine vinegar

2 tablespoons pomegranate
molasses

1 tablespoon minced shallots

¼ plus ⅛ teaspoon coarse salt,
divided

13 grinds black pepper, divided

¼ cup extra-virgin olive oil

4 cups frisée (about 1 small
bunch, core removed and
discarded and the remainder
broken up, then washed and
spun dry)

2 cups diced English cucumbers

Scant 1 cup diced tomatoes

8 pitted dates, coarsely chopped

¼ cup pomegranate seeds

2 tablespoons thinly sliced
scallions, white and light
green parts only

TO ASSEMBLE

1 cup Greek yogurt (optional)

2 tablespoons finely chopped
fresh cilantro or flat-leaf
parsley leaves, for serving
(optional)

MAKE THE HARVEST SALAD

1. In a small bowl, whisk together the vinegar, pomegranate molasses, shallots, ¼ teaspoon salt, and 5 grinds pepper. Slowly add the oil and whisk extremely well to blend. Set the dressing aside.

2. In a large salad bowl, use tongs to toss together the frisée, cucumbers, tomatoes, dates, pomegranate seeds, scallions, the remaining ⅛ teaspoon salt, and the remaining 8 grinds pepper. Rewhisk the dressing, then add ¼ cup of it to the salad; toss again.

TO SERVE

Serve the warm *jibn* topped with a dollop of yogurt and garnished with fresh cilantro or parsley leaves, if desired. Plate the salad alongside.

SERVING SUGGESTIONS: Add some toasted pita bread, then finish with date or fig cookies for dessert.

Warm Goat Cheese Salad with Strawberries and Toasted Almonds

SERVES 4, WITH ¾ CUP DRESSING

This salad balances warm, creamy breaded goat cheese rounds with fresh strawberries and crisp, slightly bitter frisée. If you like, cut the dressing recipe in half (it makes double what you need for this salad); however, I love to whip up a batch to use all week. Feel free to toast the almonds ahead and store them tightly covered for a day. Just watch them while they toast, as they burn easily (see p. 7). You can also bread the goat cheese rounds in advance, even a day ahead of time (just cover tightly in the fridge). Zest the lemon before juicing.

FOR THE HONEY-LEMON DRESSING

- ¼ cup plus 2 tablespoons canola or walnut oil
- ¼ cup fresh-squeezed, strained lemon juice
- 3 tablespoons finely chopped shallots
- 1 tablespoon plus 1 teaspoon honey
- 2 teaspoons Dijon mustard
- ½ teaspoon coarse salt
- 3 grinds black pepper

1. In a small bowl, whisk together all of the dressing ingredients until well combined.

2. Lightly grease a baking sheet with nonstick cooking spray, and heat the oven to 400°F. In a small bowl, mix together the breadcrumbs, melted butter, zest, thyme, ½ teaspoon salt, and 4 grinds pepper. With a sharp knife, cut the goat cheese log into 12 rounds. Dredge all sides of each round in the breadcrumb mixture to coat thoroughly and transfer to the baking sheet (pat on extra breading once the round is on the sheet). Chill for at least 30 minutes. Transfer to the oven and bake until golden brown, about 10 minutes.

3. While the cheese bakes, in a large bowl, use tongs to toss together the almonds, strawberries, frisée, the remaining ¼ teaspoon salt, the remaining 3 grinds pepper, and half of the dressing; divide among four plates. Top each portion with 3 warm goat cheese rounds. Serve immediately.

FOR THE SALAD

1 cup plain fresh breadcrumbs

2 tablespoons unsalted butter, melted

1 teaspoon lemon zest

½ teaspoon minced fresh thyme leaves

¾ teaspoon coarse salt, divided

7 grinds black pepper, divided

One 12-ounce log fresh goat cheese, chilled

¾ cup blanched slivered almonds, lightly toasted

20 strawberries, hulled and halved

5 ounces frisée leaves, washed and spun dry

SERVING SUGGESTION: Pair the salad with a crusty baguette and—if you're really hungry—pea soup.

TRY THIS: It's easiest to slice goat cheese right out of the fridge. To slice it, use a very sharp knife or a piece of clean dental floss (it sounds crazy but it works well). Also, chilling the breaded goat cheese rounds helps the breading adhere and prevents the cheese rounds from melting in the oven.

Roasted Beet Caprese Salad with Garlicky Black Olive Toasts

SERVES 4

Garlic oil–bathed toasts slathered with decadent black olive tapenade add richness to this light entrée. Tapenade should be easy to find; if not, use my recipe on p. 95. End your meal simply, with vanilla ice cream topped with balsamic-glazed strawberries.

1 pound 2 ounces beets

¾ cup plus 1 tablespoon extra-virgin olive oil, divided

2 tablespoons chopped garlic

¼ cup plus 1 tablespoon balsamic vinegar

2 tablespoons finely chopped shallots

1 teaspoon honey

About ¾ teaspoon coarse salt, divided

8 thin slices plain country bread

About ⅔ cup black olive tapenade (make sure it doesn't include anchovy)

5 ounces wild arugula (rocket), about 5 cups, washed and spun dry

1 pound fresh mozzarella ball, thinly sliced

About 15 grinds black pepper

About 16 large fresh basil leaves, washed and dried between paper towels

1. Heat the oven to 400°F. Wrap the beets tightly in aluminum foil, and roast until tender, about 1 hour 20 minutes. When cool enough to handle, trim, peel, and cut into ¼-inch-thick rounds. Set aside to cool. Leave the oven on.

2. In a small bowl, combine ½ cup oil with the garlic. Let sit for about 2 hours at room temperature to infuse, then strain and discard the garlic (keep the garlic oil).

3. In a small bowl, whisk together the remaining ¼ cup plus 1 tablespoon oil, the balsamic vinegar, shallots, honey, and ¼ teaspoon salt. Set the vinaigrette aside.

4. About 30 minutes before you plan to serve the salad, place the bread slices on a baking sheet. Brush with the garlic oil (you might have an extra tablespoon left over). Bake the bread until golden brown, about 10 minutes. Slather each slice with the black olive tapenade.

5. In a large bowl, use tongs to toss the arugula with ⅛ teaspoon salt and ¼ cup balsamic vinaigrette. Transfer the dressed greens to a large white platter. On a large surface, line up the roasted beet slices close together. Sprinkle evenly with ¼ teaspoon salt and 8 grinds pepper. On another large surface, line up the mozzarella slices close together. Sprinkle evenly with ⅛ teaspoon salt and 7 grinds pepper.

6. Arrange the seasoned beet slices, cheese slices, and basil leaves on the platter, overlapping them in an attractive pattern. Drizzle the mixture evenly with the remaining vinaigrette. Serve the platter with the black olive tapenade toasts, family-style.

dinner

MEATY DOESN'T HAVE TO MEAN MEAT-BASED, as you'll find in these satisfying entrées with smoky and earthy qualities. Beet (instead of beef) Wellington. Spaghetti with white bean balls (not meatballs). Tofu milanese with arugula and tomatoes (forget the usual chicken), and beet steaks roasted and drizzled with a red-wine-mushroom sauce. Roasted red peppers add sweetness and vibrancy to spanakopita. Mac and cheese gets the Spanish treatment—with Manchego, smoked paprika, and garlic-thyme breadcrumbs. And yams are formed into patties, pan-fried, and served with lemony smoked paprika mayo. You'll find panko- and seaweed-crusted tofu with a tame remoulade sauce, plus six "burgers" (everything from Indian-spiced lentil patties with mango chutney to a classic version with brown rice, mushrooms, and carrots). Who needs meat or fish?

Greek Stuffed Peppers with Lemon-Thyme Breadcrumbs

SERVES 4

Breadcrumbs on top add crunch to these hearty stuffed peppers. For a sweet touch, stir currants into the filling.

4 bell peppers (in different colors, if you like)

1 cup reduced-sodium vegetable broth

½ cup plus 2 tablespoons extra-virgin olive oil, divided

1⅛ teaspoons coarse salt, divided

1 cup couscous

1 cup finely chopped red onions

1 tablespoon finely chopped garlic, divided

4 heaping packed cups fresh spinach leaves, washed and spun dry

10 grinds black pepper

1 cup crumbled feta

Scant ¾ cup coarsely chopped pitted Kalamata olives

2 tablespoons fresh-squeezed, strained lemon juice

½ cup panko breadcrumbs

1 teaspoon minced fresh thyme leaves

1 heaping teaspoon lemon zest

1. Heat the oven to 375°F. Fill a large heavy Dutch oven two-thirds full of water and bring to a boil, covered, over high heat. Meanwhile, cut the stems and the top ½ inch off the peppers. Discard the stems and finely chop the ½ inch of flesh (you'll need 2 cups of chopped bell peppers). Remove the seeds and excess white membrane from each pepper cavity. If any peppers won't stand up easily, cut very thin slices off their bottoms (but not enough to cut into the cavities). Once the water is boiling, add the peppers and boil until they're slightly softened, about 5 minutes. With tongs, gently remove the peppers from the water and stand them upside down on a large surface to drain.

2. Add the broth, 2 tablespoons oil, and ¼ teaspoon salt to a heavy medium-sized saucepan, and bring to a boil over high heat. As soon as the mixture comes to a boil, stir in the couscous. Return the mixture to a boil, cover the pot, and remove from the heat. Let it sit, covered, for 5 minutes. Fluff with a fork.

3. Heat 2 tablespoons oil in a 12-inch, heavy, nonstick sauté pan over medium-high heat. When hot, add the 2 cups of chopped bell peppers, the red onions, and 2 teaspoons garlic and sauté until softened, about 5 minutes. Add the spinach, ½ teaspoon salt, and all of the black pepper and sauté, tossing with tongs, until the spinach is completely wilted, about 4 minutes. Using tongs, transfer the vegetable mixture to the pot of couscous. Stir in the feta, olives, lemon juice, and 2 tablespoons olive oil, and mix well.

continued

4. Grease a medium-large baking dish with 1 tablespoon oil; place the baking dish on a baking sheet. Stand the peppers, top up, in the dish. Drizzle them evenly with a total of 1 tablespoon oil. Sprinkle them evenly with a total of ¼ teaspoon salt. Stuff the peppers with the couscous-vegetable mixture. Pack it in tightly and let it overflow—press down gently so it stays in each pepper. Transfer the dish to the oven and cook, uncovered, until the peppers are very tender and hot, about 25 minutes.

5. Meanwhile, heat the remaining 2 tablespoons oil over medium heat in a small, heavy, nonstick sauté pan. Once hot, add the remaining 1 teaspoon garlic and sauté until softened and aromatic, no more than 1 minute. Stir in the breadcrumbs and ⅛ teaspoon salt and cook, stirring occasionally, until lightly golden brown, 2 to 3 minutes. Stir in the thyme and lemon zest. When the peppers come out of the oven, divide the breadcrumb topping over each pepper, and serve.

SERVING SUGGESTIONS: Accompany the peppers with tzatziki (Greek cucumber-yogurt dip) and warm pita bread. Set out baklava for dessert.

TRY THIS:

* Since the membranes in bell peppers can be bitter, it's best to remove them. To do so, use a small paring knife to cut gently down the interior sides. Or, snip them off with kitchen shears.
* Instead of boiling the peppers as in Step 1 on p. 115, microwave them.

Veggie Chili with Butternut Squash

SERVES 6 TO 8; MAKES ABOUT 9 CUPS

Vibrant and vegetable-rich, this stew is vegan if not accompanied by sour cream or cheese. You'll definitely want to prepare a large batch to have enough for dinner and leftovers!

2 tablespoons vegetable oil

4 cups small-dice peeled butternut squash

1½ cups finely chopped red onions

1½ cups finely chopped green bell peppers

1¼ cups finely chopped carrots

⅓ cup finely chopped scallions, white, light green, and a couple of inches of darker green parts

1 tablespoon plus 1 teaspoon finely chopped garlic

1 tablespoon plus 1 teaspoon finely chopped jalapeños (seeds and membranes removed)

One 15-ounce can pinto beans, rinsed and drained

One 15-ounce can kidney beans, rinsed and drained

4 to 5 tablespoons tomato paste

1 tablespoon coarse salt

2 teaspoons ground cumin

1 teaspoon ancho chile powder

1 teaspoon dried oregano

5 grinds black pepper

2 cups reduced-sodium vegetable stock

¾ cup strained canned tomatoes, preferably Muir Glen

Scant ¼ cup fresh-squeezed, strained lime juice

FOR SERVING

Chopped fresh cilantro leaves

Sour cream

Shredded Cheddar or Monterey Jack

Diced avocado

Tortilla chips

1. Heat the oil in a large, heavy Dutch oven over medium-high heat. When hot, add the squash, onions, bell peppers, carrots, scallions, garlic, and jalapeños, and sauté until the onions are soft and the other vegetables are beginning to soften, about 10 minutes. Stir in the pinto beans, kidney beans, tomato paste, salt, cumin, chile powder, oregano, and black pepper, and cook for another 3 minutes. Add the stock, tomatoes, and lime juice, and simmer until the squash and carrots are completely tender, another 15 to 20 minutes.

2. Serve while hot, topping with cilantro, sour cream, cheese, and avocado, with chips on the side.

SERVING SUGGESTIONS: Offer cornbread or brown rice alongside, with cinnamon hot chocolate for dessert.

Whole Wheat Linguini with Oven-Roasted Tomatoes, Broccoli, White Beans, and Pine Nuts

SERVES 4

When I was a child, my father would make me and my sister spaghetti with broccoli, pine nuts, and Parmesan (the type in the small green can). Here's an improved version of this childhood favorite—with whole wheat pasta for healthfulness, lots of freshly grated Parmigiano-Reggiano, and white beans for added protein. The oven-roasted tomatoes add sweetness and juiciness. Plan ahead, as the tomatoes take several hours.

8 plum tomatoes, cored and halved vertically

¼ cup plus 1 teaspoon extra-virgin olive oil, divided

2 teaspoons finely chopped garlic

1⅛ teaspoons coarse salt, plus extra for salting the pasta water, divided

A scant ½ teaspoon black pepper

8 ounces whole wheat linguini

5 scant cups 1- to 1½-inch broccoli florets (from 1 bunch)

½ cup pine nuts

One 15-ounce can white beans, rinsed and drained

¾ packed cup freshly grated Parmigiano-Reggiano

1 heaping teaspoon lemon zest

1. Heat the oven to 250°F. Place the tomatoes cut side up on a foil-lined baking sheet with sides. Drizzle with ¼ cup oil and sprinkle evenly with the garlic, ¾ teaspoon salt, and about ¼ teaspoon pepper. Roast until the tomatoes are shriveled but still retain some juices, 3½ to 4 hours.

2. While the tomatoes roast, fill a medium-sized saucepan two-thirds full of heavily salted water, cover, and bring to a boil over high heat. When the water is boiling, stir in the pasta and boil, stirring occasionally, until al dente, about 8 minutes (follow the package directions). Drain in a colander set in the sink.

3. Meanwhile, add about 1½ inches of water to another medium-sized saucepan, cover, and bring to a boil over high heat. Once boiling, add a steamer insert, place the broccoli florets in the insert, cover the pot, and reduce the heat to medium low. Steam until the broccoli is tender yet still a bit crisp and bright green, about 11 minutes. Set aside off the heat.

continued

4. Heat the remaining 1 teaspoon oil in a small heavy sauté pan over medium heat. When warm, add the nuts and ⅛ teaspoon salt, and toast until golden brown, 2 to 3 minutes (watch very carefully, as pine nuts burn easily). Immediately pour the nuts onto a plate and set aside.

5. Transfer the oven-roasted tomatoes and all of their juices to a large bowl, then add the hot drained pasta, steamed broccoli, toasted nuts, drained beans, cheese, and lemon zest. Add the remaining ¼ teaspoon salt and the remaining pepper and toss gently with tongs. Serve immediately.

SERVING SUGGESTIONS: Serve the pasta with an arugula and avocado salad, with a berry tart for dessert.

TRY THIS: To save time, substitute drained sun-dried tomatoes (packed in oil) for the oven-roasted tomatoes.

MAKE IT VEGAN: To convert this dish to vegan, use non-dairy cheese such as Go Veggie!™ Grated Parmesan Style Topping.

Fried Eggplant-Hummus Sandwiches with Pickled Carrots and Radishes

SERVES 6; MAKES ABOUT 2½ CUPS HUMMUS

Inspired by the Mideastern dish *sabich*, these fork-and-knife sandwiches take a couple of hours to prepare, but are completely worth it. Filled with crispy, meaty eggplant, creamy and tangy hummus, rich and tender hard-cooked eggs, and sweet and slightly crunchy pickled vegetables, they're extremely satisfying. The eggplant can be served hot, room temperature, or cold. There's no need to salt the eggplant, but be sure to peel the tough, slightly bitter skin. To save time, use store-bought hummus and pickles.

10 large eggs, divided

2 medium eggplants, trimmed, peeled, and sliced ½ inch thick (about 22 rounds)

1½ teaspoons coarse salt, divided

A scant ¾ teaspoon black pepper, divided

1 cup unbleached all-purpose flour

1 cup panko breadcrumbs

1 cup plain whole wheat breadcrumbs

⅛ teaspoon crushed red pepper flakes

1 cup extra-virgin olive oil for frying, divided

12 slices high-quality country bread

Herbed Hummus (recipe on p. 122)

Quick-Pickled Carrots and Radishes (on p. 123)

1. Place 6 eggs in the bottom of a medium-sized, heavy saucepan and cover by 1 inch of water; cover with a lid and bring to a full boil over high heat. Once the water comes to a boil, turn off the heat and place the pot on a cool burner. Cover and let sit for 12 minutes (set the timer). Meanwhile, fill a large bowl with ice water and place a colander in the sink. After 12 minutes, drain the eggs into the colander, and then transfer them to the bowl of ice water. Let sit for a couple of minutes, and then carefully peel the eggs. Halve each one vertically and set aside.

2. Place the eggplant rounds on a large baking sheet or cutting board and evenly season the sides facing up with a total of ½ teaspoon salt and ¼ teaspoon black pepper; turn over the eggplant and season evenly with a total of ½ teaspoon salt and ¼ teaspoon pepper.

3. In a medium-sized bowl, combine the flour with ¼ teaspoon salt and 10 grinds pepper; mix well. In another medium-sized bowl, whisk the remaining 4 eggs until smooth. In a large bowl, mix together the panko, whole wheat breadcrumbs, ¼ teaspoon salt, the remaining black pepper, and ⅛ teaspoon red pepper flakes. Set up an assembly line: first the eggplant, then the flour, then the eggs, and finally the breadcrumb mixture.

continued

4. Using tongs, coat both sides of each eggplant round in the flour, shaking off excess. Then dip both sides in the egg to cover. Then coat both sides in the breadcrumbs to cover. Set the breaded rounds aside on a baking sheet.

5. Add ¼ cup oil to each of two medium-sized, heavy, nonstick frying pans and heat over medium. When the oil is hot but not smoking, add a quarter of the eggplant to each pan. Cook until the sides facing down are golden brown and crisp, about 4 minutes. Turn and cook until the other sides are golden brown and crisp, about another 4 minutes. Transfer to a clean cutting board, cover, and set aside. Add another ¼ cup oil to each of the pans and divide the remaining eggplant slices between them. Brown both sides, about another 7 or 8 minutes total. Transfer to the cutting board, cover, and set aside.

6. Toast the bread until lightly golden brown. Slather 2 tablespoons of the Herbed Hummus on each of 6 slices. Sprinkle a scant tablespoon of the Quick-Pickled Carrots and Radishes (make sure to drain them well first) over top. Arrange 3 to 4 eggplant rounds and 2 egg halves on top of each. Cover with the remaining bread slices. Slice each sandwich in half, and serve.

HERBED HUMMUS

MAKES ABOUT 2½ CUPS

3 medium garlic cloves

One 26½-ounce can chickpeas, rinsed and drained

¼ cup plus 2 tablespoons fresh flat-leaf parsley leaves

¼ cup fresh-squeezed, strained lemon juice

3 tablespoons tahini paste

1½ teaspoons coarse salt

½ teaspoon cumin

¼ teaspoon coriander

⅛ teaspoon Aleppo pepper or crushed red pepper flakes

10 grinds black pepper

¾ cup extra-virgin olive oil

Place the garlic in the bowl of the food processor and process until finely chopped, about 5 seconds. Add the remaining ingredients except for the oil and purée until well mixed, about 15 seconds. Add the oil and process until smooth, about another 40 seconds.

QUICK-PICKLED CARROTS AND RADISHES

MAKES ABOUT 1½ CUPS

1 cup cider vinegar

¼ cup plus 1 tablespoon
granulated sugar

½ teaspoon coarse salt

¼ teaspoon whole coriander
seeds

⅛ teaspoon whole yellow
mustard seeds

15 whole black peppercorns

8 whole cloves

4 radishes, trimmed, quartered,
and thinly sliced

1 medium carrot, peeled, halved
vertically, and thinly sliced

Add the first seven ingredients plus 1 cup water to a small heavy saucepan, and bring to a boil over high heat, stirring to help the sugar dissolve. Boil until the flavor is concentrated, about 10 minutes. Add the radishes and carrots to a medium-sized bowl and pour the hot vinegar mixture over them; let sit until the pickles reach room temperature.

SERVING SUGGESTIONS: Begin with a chopped tomato and cucumber salad with pomegranate vinaigrette, and finish the meal with halvah (similar to fudge and made with sesame seeds) and ripe apricots.

Bean Loaf with Maple Cranberry Sauce

SERVES 8

This substantial entrée is ideal for Thanksgiving or dinner during the colder months. Loaded with harvest flavor, the tender slices taste just like traditional turkey meatloaf. The accompanying tart-sweet cranberry sauce—full of deep flavor from the maple syrup—gilds the lily. For a kid-friendly presentation or format appropriate for parties, bake the mixture in muffin pans. ❡ Don't be intimidated by the long ingredient list—the dish is simple to prepare and ideal for leftovers. Be sure to purchase peeled and roasted chestnuts for ease. They're a bit pricey, but well worth it for their sweet, nutty flavor and silken, meaty texture.

3 thin slices sourdough bread

1 cup 2% milk

2 cups peeled, cored, and chopped, sweet-tart apples, such as Macintosh

18 peeled and roasted whole chestnuts, such as Minerva brand, chopped

One 15-ounce can cannellini (white) beans, rinsed and drained

One 15-ounce can pinto beans, rinsed and drained

2½ tablespoons unsalted butter, divided

1 packed tablespoon coarsely chopped garlic

1 cup coarsely chopped red onions

1 cup coarsely chopped celery

8 ounces white button mushrooms, coarsely chopped

1. Heat the oven to 350°F. In a large bowl, mash together the bread and milk with your hands to form a damp, crumbly mixture (you should yield 1½ cups); add the apples, chestnuts, cannellini beans, and pinto beans.

2. Heat 2 tablespoons of the butter over medium-high heat in a 10-inch, heavy, nonstick sauté pan. Once melted, add the garlic, onions, and celery, and sauté until softened, about 5 minutes. Add the mushrooms and continue sautéing until they're very tender, about another 9 minutes. Add the sautéed vegetables to the bread-apple-bean mixture. Stir in the sage, mustard, maple syrup, rosemary, salt, and pepper.

3. Transfer this mixture to the bowl of a food processor, and purée until well combined and smooth, using a rubber spatula to scrape down the sides of the bowl occasionally, about 1 minute total (if necessary, do this in two batches). Pour the puréed mixture back into the bowl you used for the bread and milk. Add the beaten egg and breadcrumbs, and mix well with your hands until well blended (the resulting mixture should look like pâté or mousseline).

3½ ounces shiitake mushrooms, stems discarded and caps coarsely chopped

20 fresh sage leaves

2 tablespoons Djion mustard

1 tablespoon maple syrup

1 tablespoon fresh rosemary sprigs

1 tablespoon coarse salt

10 grinds black pepper

1 large egg, beaten

1 cup whole wheat panko breadcrumbs

Maple Cranberry Sauce (recipe below)

4. With the remaining ½ tablespoon of butter, grease the entire inside of aan 8½ x 4¼ x 3-inch loaf pan. Pour in the mixture and pat down to flatten (it should reach up to the top). Transfer the pan to the oven and bake until the loaf is set and slightly crisp on top, about 40 minutes. Let sit at room temperature for 15 minutes before cutting into eight slices. Serve each slice with some cranberry sauce.

MAPLE CRANBERRY SAUCE

MAKES 1½ CUPS

One 12-ounce bag fresh cranberries

½ cup maple syrup

¼ cup fresh-squeezed, strained orange juice

Scant ½ teaspoon minced fresh rosemary

Scant ¼ teaspoon coarse salt

Add all of the ingredients plus ¼ cup of water to a small heavy saucepan, and bring to a boil over high heat. Once boiling, reduce the heat to medium and simmer until a thick, soft sauce with just a few remaining whole berries forms, about 8 minutes. Let cool to room temperature.

SERVING SUGGESTIONS: Serve the duo with crispy roasted potatoes or mashed potatoes and sautéed greens. Cap the meal with apple crisp.

Mexican Pinto Bean Burgers with Fresh Guacamole and Corn Pico de Gallo

SERVES 4; MAKES ABOUT 1½ CUPS GUACAMOLE AND ¾ CUP PICO DE GALLO

These burgers can be vegan if you use a soy Cheddar. If you're not a fan of cilantro, swap in fresh parsley leaves. ¶ For ease, prepare the condiments before whipping up the burgers. Use a not-too-ripe tomato in the guacamole so the fruit holds together once you remove the seeds. Prepare the guac right before serving and cover it with a piece of aluminum foil or plastic wrap pressed down on the surface to prevent browning. Wearing rubber gloves makes mincing the jalapeño more comfortable. Unlike the tomato for the guacamole, choose a ripe, juicy one for the pico de gallo.

FOR THE GUACAMOLE

2 ripe avocados

½ cup diced tomatoes (seeds removed)

¼ cup finely chopped red onions

2 tablespoons finely chopped fresh cilantro leaves

2 tablespoons fresh-squeezed, strained lime juice

1 teaspoon minced jalapeños (seeds and membranes removed)

½ teaspoon coarse salt

5 grinds black pepper

FOR THE CORN PICO DE GALLO

¾ cup diced tomato (with seeds)

¼ cup corn kernels (if frozen, thawed and drained)

2 tablespoons finely chopped red onions

1 tablespoon fresh-squeezed, strained lime juice

continued

MAKE THE GUACAMOLE

Combine all of the ingredients in a medium bowl and set aside.

MAKE THE PICO DE GALLO

Combine all of the ingredients in a medium bowl and set aside.

MAKE THE PINTO BEAN BURGERS

1. Combine the first 12 ingredients in the bowl of a food processor; purée until the mixture comes together, about 20 seconds. Turn out into a bowl, and gently knead with your hands. Form the mixture into four ½-inch-thick patties and indent the center of each a bit with your fingers.

2. Heat half of the oil in a 12-inch, heavy, nonstick sauté pan over medium-high heat. When hot, add the burgers and cook until golden brown on both sides, turning over halfway through and using the remaining oil when the pan gets dry, about 8 minutes total.

3. Place a patty on half of each bun. Top each patty with a couple of tablespoons of guacamole and about 1½ tablespoons of pico de gallo. Serve immediately.

continued

1 tablespoon finely chopped
fresh cilantro leaves

⅛ teaspoon coarse salt

3 grinds black pepper

FOR THE MEXICAN PINTO BEAN
BURGERS

One 15-ounce can pinto beans,
rinsed and drained

1 cup panko breadcrumbs

¼ cup shredded mild Cheddar

¼ cup finely chopped red
onions

1 tablespoon finely chopped
fresh cilantro leaves

1 tablespoon ketchup

1 tablespoon liquid from canned
chipotle chiles en adobo

¾ teaspoon coarse salt, divided

½ teaspoon ground cumin

5 grinds black pepper, divided

⅛ teaspoon ancho chile powder

⅛ teaspoon ground coriander

About ¼ cup vegetable oil,
divided

4 burger buns, split and toasted

SERVING SUGGESTIONS: Loaded with flavor, these burgers would pair well with watermelon slices squeezed with fresh lime and sprinkled with chile powder; a margarita or limeade alongside wouldn't hurt. For dessert, try Mexican chocolate brownies (brownies with vanilla and cinnamon).

TRY THIS: Removing the seeds from tomatoes for guacamole is a must—you don't want wet, gloppy seeds in the creamy dip! Here's how to do it: Use a serrated knife to slice each tomato in half crosswise. Then, over the sink, gently squeeze out the seeds. Alternatively, use your fingers to scrape them out.

Rustic Vegetable Tart with Roasted Butternut Squash, Parsnips, and Brussels Sprouts

SERVES 4 TO 6

I came up with this rich autumnal tart when I wanted to use leftover ingredients from preparing Thanksgiving dinner. In fact, this dish could star as the centerpiece of Thanksgiving dinner or any festive meal on a cold evening. Make sure to wash the leeks well and to cool the filling ingredients to room temperature before placing them on the dough round.

2 cups plus 3 tablespoons unbleached all-purpose flour, divided

1 tablespoon minced fresh sage leaves

About 1½ teaspoons coarse salt, divided, plus extra for salting the water

5 tablespoons (½ stick plus 1 tablespoon) unsalted butter, 3 tablespoons diced and chilled, divided

3 tablespoons trans-fat-free vegetable shortening, chilled

2 cups ¼-inch-thick slices peeled butternut squash

1½ cups ¼-inch-thick slices peeled parsnips

3 tablespoons extra-virgin olive oil, divided

12 grinds black pepper, divided

2 cups trimmed and quartered large Brussels sprouts

continued

1. Heat the oven to 400°F.

2. In a large bowl, whisk together 2 cups plus 2 tablespoons of the flour, all of the sage, and ½ teaspoon salt. Add the 3 tablespoons of chilled butter and all of the shortening. Use your fingers to crumble and massage the ingredients together until they are well mixed and the consistency of coarse meal. Pour in 6 tablespoons of ice water (just the water, not the ice) and very gently knead the mixture together. As soon as the dough comes together, stop kneading and adding water (don't overknead the dough or it will become tough and lose its flakiness). You might need another 3 tablespoons of ice water, for a total of ½ cup plus 1 tablespoon ice water.

3. Form the dough into a ball and place it on a large piece of plastic wrap; cover completely with the plastic wrap and flatten the ball into a circle. Refrigerate for about an hour.

4. Meanwhile, transfer the butternut squash and parsnip slices to a baking sheet with sides and toss with 2 tablespoons oil, ½ teaspoon salt, and 8 grinds pepper. Mix well with your hands and then roast until tender and golden brown, about 20 minutes. Let cool to room temperature (to expedite this, carefully transfer the roasted vegetables to a plate). Reduce the oven temperature to 375°F.

5. While the squash and parsnips roast, fill a medium-sized, heavy saucepot two-thirds full of heavily salted water, cover, and bring to a boil over high heat. Once the water is boiling, add the Brussels sprouts, stir, and cook until the vegetables

continued

2 cups thinly sliced leeks
cut into half-moons

½ cup freshly grated
Parmigiano-Reggiano

½ cup freshly grated Gruyère

1 large egg

2 teaspoons white truffle oil
(optional)

are bright green and tender, about 5 minutes. Use a spider or slotted spoon to drain the vegetables well and transfer them to a bowl. Add 1 tablespoon oil, ⅛ teaspoon salt, and 4 grinds pepper, and toss well. Let cool to room temperature.

6. Add the remaining 2 tablespoons butter to a 10-inch, heavy sauté pan, and heat over medium. Once the butter has melted, add the leeks and ¼ teaspoon salt; stir and sauté until the leeks are very tender, sweet, and just beginning to become very light golden brown in spots, about 8 minutes. Let cool to room temperature (to expedite this, you can place the leeks on a plate and refrigerate).

7. Sprinkle the remaining 1 tablespoon flour onto a cold, large, clean surface. Unwrap the chilled dough and transfer to the surface. With a very lightly floured rolling pin, roll out the dough into a ⅛-inch-thick circle about 12 or 13 inches in diameter. Transfer to a parchment-lined baking sheet. Evenly sprinkle the center of the dough with Parmigiano-Reggiano (leave a border of 2 to 3 inches all around). On top, evenly sprinkle the leeks (leaving the same border). On top of the leeks, arrange the Brussels sprouts (leaving the same border). Then place the squash and parsnips on top, evenly distributing them, and sprinkle with the Gruyère, leaving the same border.

8. Fold the edges of the dough over the outer couple of inches of the filling all around in a circle, making a rustic pastry border. Patch holes or weak spots with any excess dough. In a small bowl, whisk together the egg with 1 tablespoon of water. With a pastry brush, brush any exposed dough. Chill the tart in the fridge for 20 minutes.

9. Bake the tart until the pastry turns light golden brown, about 45 minutes. Drizzle the filling evenly with the truffle oil, if desired. Let the tart cool for 10 to 15 minutes, then slice and serve.

SERVING SUGGESTIONS: Serve slices alongside braised red cabbage and apples or a salad of radicchio and apple. Poached pears with cinnamon crème fraîche would be an ideal dessert.

Steamed Vegetable and Tofu Dumplings

SERVES 8; MAKES ABOUT 50 DUMPLINGS AND ¾ CUP DIPPING SAUCE

I'm slightly obsessed with dim sum, especially these steamed vegan dumplings. These are tender and full of flavor (enough so that you can even skip the sauce). In addition to dinner, they'd be ideal for a party (cover cooked dumplings to keep them warm while you prepare the remainder). ❡ Look for wonton wrappers in the refrigerated section of the grocery store (usually near the tofu). To save time, assemble the first 12 dumplings and put together the remainder once the steaming process has begun. You can also prepare the filling a day before assembling and cooking the dumplings. Feel free to purchase bagged shredded carrots and to roughly chop the vegetables and tofu.

FOR THE DUMPLINGS

3 tablespoons vegetable oil, divided

¼ cup thinly sliced scallions, white and light green parts only

1 tablespoon minced peeled fresh ginger

2 teaspoons minced garlic

2 cups shredded carrots

8 ounces white button mushrooms, trimmed and cut into small dice

1 head bok choy, stalk and leaves finely chopped separately, divided

¼ cup reduced-sodium soy sauce

3 tablespoons reduced-sodium vegetable stock

1 tablespoon light brown sugar

2 teaspoons toasted sesame oil

¼ plus ⅛ teaspoon coarse salt

⅛ teaspoon Sriracha

MAKE THE DUMPLINGS

1. Heat 1 tablespoon oil in a 10-inch heavy sauté pan over medium-high heat. When hot, add the scallions, ginger, and garlic, and sauté until softened, about 2 minutes. Add the carrots, mushrooms, and bok choy stalk, and sauté until softened and reduced in volume, about 5 minutes. Add the soy sauce, stock, sugar, sesame oil, salt, and Sriracha sauce and simmer, stirring, for 3 minutes. Add the bok choy leaves and tofu and continue to simmer, stirring occasionally, until all of the liquid has been absorbed and the vegetables are very soft, about another 15 minutes. (You should yield a scant 4 cups of filling.) Immediately chill in the refrigerator or freezer until the mixture reaches room temperature (or colder), about 10 minutes.

2. Line up the wonton wrappers on a large, clean surface. Pour some water into a small bowl. Using a pastry brush, brush the edges of the wrappers with water. Spoon about 1½ teaspoons of the vegetable filling onto the center of each wrapper. Fold the top half of each wrapper over the bottom to form a triangle. Press down on the sides to form a tight seal. Then, fold the two equal sides of the triangle toward the center of each triangle to form a small bundle. Repeat with all of the wrappers, water, and filling.

12 ounces extra-firm tofu, cut into small dice

One 12-ounce package wonton wrappers

FOR THE DIPPING SAUCE

¼ cup reduced-sodium soy sauce

¼ cup reduced-sodium vegetable broth

2 tablespoons toasted sesame oil

2 tablespoons thinly sliced scallions, white and light green parts only

1 tablespoon light brown sugar

2 teaspoons unseasoned rice vinegar

3. Brush a steamer insert and large baking sheet with the remaining 2 tablespoons of oil. Pour about 2 inches of water into a medium-sized saucepan. Add the greased insert, cover with a lid, and bring the water to a boil over high heat. Once the water is boiling, place about 12 dumplings on the steamer insert. Cover and steam until the dumpling dough is tender, about 7 minutes. Transfer the cooked dumplings to the greased baking sheet. Repeat with the remaining dumplings.

MAKE THE DIPPING SAUCE

Combine all of the sauce ingredients in a medium bowl. Serve with the hot dumplings.

SERVING SUGGESTION: Serve with ginger-sautéed spinach and cold sesame noodles, with lychee fruit for dessert.

TRY THIS: If you're craving crispy fare, pan-fry the dumplings: Start with 2 tablespoons of vegetable oil in a nonstick skillet set on medium high. The dumplings develop a golden brown color after about 3 minutes per side.

Roasted Indian-Spiced Vegetables and Chickpeas with Raisins

SERVES 4 TO 5

This quick and easy vegan entrée is economical and crowd-pleasing. Seek out garam masala (Indian spice blend) without salt, and prep the other ingredients while the potatoes roast.

28 ounces baby red potatoes, quartered

½ cup vegetable oil, divided

2 teaspoons coarse salt, divided

5 grinds black pepper

1 pound carrots, peeled and cut into 2- x ½-inch matchsticks

1 small head cauliflower, cut into 1-inch florets

½ cup raisins or currants

One 15-ounce can chickpeas, rinsed and drained

½ cup finely chopped fresh flat-leaf parsley or cilantro leaves

1 tablespoon fresh-squeezed, strained lemon juice

1 teaspoon garam masala (without salt)

About 2 cups plain soy yogurt, for serving

1. Place two oven racks in the top two-thirds of the oven. Place a rimmed baking sheet on the top rack and heat the oven to 400°F. Once the oven is hot, carefully remove the hot pan. Using tongs, toss the potatoes well with half of the oil, ½ teaspoon salt, and all of the pepper. Roast until the potatoes are tender and golden brown and crispy in many parts, about 50 minutes, tossing halfway through.

2. On another rimmed baking sheet, toss the carrots, 2 tablespoons oil, and ½ teaspoon salt; spread on one side of the pan and roast for 15 minutes (put this pan on the lower oven rack); remove the baking sheet from the oven and use a spatula to flip over the carrots. Onto the empty half of the baking sheet, use tongs to toss the cauliflower florets, the remaining 2 tablespoons oil, and ½ teaspoon salt. Keep the carrots and cauliflower separate as best as possible. Return the pan to the oven and roast the carrots and cauliflower until both are tender when poked with a fork and golden brown in a few spots, about another 20 minutes.

3. Meanwhile, place the raisins in a small bowl and cover with ½ cup of boiling or very hot water. Let sit until the raisins are tender, about 30 minutes, then drain.

4. Pour the potatoes, carrots, and cauliflower (with their oil) into a large bowl, then add the drained raisins, drained chickpeas, parsley, lemon juice, garam masala, and the remaining ½ teaspoon salt. Toss well with tongs. Divide among the serving plates and add a dollop of soy yogurt alongside each portion.

SERVING SUGGESTION: Finish your meal very simply by setting out ripe and juicy mango slices.

Spanish Yam-wiches with Lemony Smoked Paprika Mayonnaise

SERVES 4

These sandwiches (vegan if you use a vegan mayonnaise) were inspired by the flavors of Spain. If you want to serve them as sliders, shape the mixture into eight patties and cook for a slightly shorter period of time; serve on slider buns.

1½ pounds red garnet yams

One 15-ounce can cannellini beans, rinsed and drained

3½ tablespoons chopped shallots

3 tablespoons finely chopped fresh flat-leaf parsley leaves

1½ teaspoons coarse salt, divided

1½ teaspoons pimentón de la Vera (dulce or sweet, Spanish smoked paprika), divided

½ teaspoon ground cumin

8 grinds black pepper

¾ cup panko breadcrumbs

½ cup mayonnaise

1 heaping teaspoon lemon zest

1 teaspoon Dijon mustard

½ cup extra-virgin olive oil, divided

4 potato buns, split and toasted

1 cup frisée, washed, spun dry, and torn into bite-sized pieces

1. Poke the yams all over with the tip of a knife. Place in the microwave and cook on high until very soft, anywhere from 8 to 16 minutes, depending on your microwave. Set aside to cool, then slice in half and scoop out the flesh. Measure out 2 cups flesh and transfer to a medium-sized bowl. Add the beans, shallots, parsley, 1 teaspoon salt, ¾ teaspoon paprika, cumin, and the black pepper. Use a potato masher to mash all of the ingredients together, and then knead with your hands to combine them well. Form into four ½-inch-thick patties.

2. Pour the panko, the remaining ½ teaspoon salt, and ¼ teaspoon smoked paprika into a medium-sized bowl and mix well. Dredge each patty in the mixture to coat both sides. Place the patties on a plate and refrigerate for 30 minutes.

3. In a small bowl, mix together the mayo, lemon zest, mustard, and the remaining ½ teaspoon paprika. Set aside.

4. Heat half of the oil in a 12-inch, heavy, nonstick sauté pan over medium-high heat. When hot, add the patties and cook until the first side is a bit crisp and very lightly golden brown, about 5 minutes (if the pan becomes dry, add another 2 tablespoons oil). Carefully flip with a silicone spatula and cook until the other side is similarly done, about another 5 minutes, adding another 2 tablespoons oil if the pan becomes dry.

5. Place a patty on the bottom of each bun, top with about 2 tablespoons paprika mayo and ¼ cup frisée, and serve.

SERVING SUGGESTIONS: Serve with roasted asparagus with lemon zest as a side, and sea-salt-chocolate bars with fresh figs for dessert.

Roasted Red Pepper and Olive Calzone with Marinara Dipping Sauce

SERVES 4

This meal captures the flavors and flag colors of Italy. Serve with an avocado and fennel salad with lemon vinaigrette and end with berry sorbet.

¼ cup extra-virgin olive oil, divided

1 ball fresh refrigerated pizza dough, whole wheat or white (about 20 ounces)

Scant 1 tablespoon minced garlic

About ⅛ teaspoon crushed red pepper flakes, divided

One 28-ounce can strained tomatoes, such as Muir Glen

1¾ teaspoons finely chopped fresh oregano leaves, divided

½ plus ⅛ teaspoon coarse salt, divided

3 grinds black pepper

1¼ cups whole milk ricotta

½ cup freshly grated Parmigiano-Reggiano

10 ounces roasted red peppers, cut in strips

20 pitted Kalamata olives

15 large fresh basil leaves, cut into chiffonade

1. Drizzle a large bowl with about 1 tablespoon oil, then place the ball of dough inside. Cover with a kitchen towel, and let sit for 1 to 2 hours at room temperature.

2. Meanwhile, heat the oven to 400°F. Heat 1 tablespoon oil in a medium-sized, heavy saucepan over medium-high heat. When the oil is hot, add the garlic and a pinch of red pepper flakes and sauté until aromatic, no more than 1 minute. Add the tomatoes, ¾ teaspoon oregano, ½ teaspoon salt, and the pepper; simmer until the flavors come together and the sauce has thickened, 15 minutes. Set the marinara sauce aside off the heat to cool just a bit.

3. In a medium bowl, stir together the two cheeses, the remaining 1 teaspoon oregano, the remaining ⅛ teaspoon salt, and a pinch of red pepper flakes. Pat the roasted red peppers and olives repeatedly with a clean kitchen towel, drying them thoroughly.

4. Brush a baking sheet with 1 tablespoon oil. Turn out the pizza dough onto a clean surface, and use a bench scraper to cut it into four equal-sized pieces. Use your hands to stretch each piece into a round with a roughly 6-inch diameter. Dollop a quarter of the cheese mixture into the center of each round, then top with a quarter of the pepper strips and olives. Fold the top part of the dough over the filling to form a half moon, and tightly seal the edges by crimping or pressing (patch any holes or weak spots with excess dough). Transfer all four raw calzones to the greased baking sheet, and brush their tops with the remaining 1 tablespoon oil.

5. Bake until the calzones puff and turn golden brown, about 20 minutes. Let cool for about 5 minutes, then sprinkle with the basil and serve with the marinara dipping sauce.

Miso-Glazed Tofu

SERVES 4

This quick vegan recipe was inspired by acclaimed chef Nobu Matsuhisa's black cod with miso—with tofu standing in for the fish. The portions are hefty, so you might have leftovers.

Two 1-pound packages extra-firm plain tofu, cut widthwise into roughly ¾-inch-thick slices (16 total)

¼ cup mirin

¼ cup sake

⅔ cup red miso paste

¼ cup plus 2 tablespoons granulated sugar

1 tablespoon plus 1 teaspoon reduced-sodium soy sauce

¼ teaspoon Sriracha or other hot sauce

½ teaspoon coarse salt, divided

14 grinds black pepper, divided

2 tablespoons vegetable oil, plus more as needed

1. Overlap paper towels to form two layers on a baking sheet. Add the sliced tofu and cover with another two layers of paper towels and another baking sheet. Let drain at room temperature for 20 minutes.

2. Meanwhile, add the mirin and sake to a small heavy saucepan, and bring to a boil over high heat. Immediately reduce the heat to medium, and add the miso paste, sugar, soy sauce, and Sriracha. Cook, whisking constantly, for about 4 minutes (the mixture will bubble and smell a bit like caramel). The goals are to cook off some of the alcohol, caramelize the sauce a bit, and completely dissolve the sugar and remove the granularity of the miso. Pour the sauce into a 9 x 13 x 2-inch glass baking dish, using a rubber spatula to scrape out any remaining marinade.

3. Let the marinade sit until it's cool enough to handle, about 3 minutes. Then add the drained tofu slices and carefully turn, coating all sides extremely well. Let sit at room temperature for 30 minutes.

4. Scrape the marinade off of the tofu and back into the baking dish (reserve the baking dish with the marinade; you will use it later on). Line up the tofu slices and sprinkle one side evenly with a total of ¼ teaspoon salt and 7 grinds pepper. Turn over and season the other side of the tofu with the remaining salt and pepper.

5. Place a large grill pan over medium-high heat; brush with vegetable oil. Place one-half to two-thirds of the tofu on the grill and cook until the first side has grill marks, about 2 minutes (watch carefully; due to its high sugar content, tofu can easily burn). Flip and cook until the remaining side has grill marks, about another 2 minutes. Transfer to the baking dish with marinade, and repeat with the remaining tofu. (For grill marks, always set the tofu down on the grill at an angle. Turn 180 degrees after 1 minute on one side and then flip over; repeat after a minute on that other side.)

6. Using tongs, gently turn the tofu in the marinade to thoroughly recoat all sides. Serve immediately.

SERVING SUGGESTIONS: Serve this dish with short-grain brown rice and stir-fried snow peas or bok choy. Non-dairy green tea ice cream would be an apt dessert.

TRY THIS: If you have leftover, marinated tofu, use it in salads and sandwiches. Slice and serve over a cold Asian noodle salad (preferably one with lots of acidity to balance the rich, sweet marinated tofu), or include in a baguette along with pickled carrots and daikon and some fresh watercress.

Whole Wheat Rigatoni with Asparagus, Leeks, and Lemony Goat Cheese

This colorful springtime pasta dish is rich, creamy, and luxurious—but healthful, too, thanks to 2% milk and whole grain pasta. Feel free to substitute sugar snap peas or snow peas for the asparagus and other pasta shapes, such as bowties or spirals, for the rigatoni.

½ teaspoon coarse salt plus a few tablespoons for salting the pasta water, divided

1 pound whole wheat rigatoni

1 bunch thin (¼-inch-thick) asparagus, bottom 2½ to 3 inches trimmed off and discarded and the remainder cut into 1-inch-long pieces

3 tablespoons unsalted butter

1 leek, ends trimmed and white and light green parts quartered, thinly sliced, and well rinsed

3 tablespoons unbleached all-purpose flour

1½ cups 2% milk, at room temperature

¼ cup minced fresh chives, divided

2 heaping teaspoons lemon zest, divided

¼ teaspoon freshly grated nutmeg

5 grinds black pepper

8 ounces soft fresh goat cheese

½ cup freshly grated Parmigiano-Reggiano

1. Fill a large, heavy saucepan two-thirds full of water and season with a few tablespoons salt. Cover and bring to a boil over high heat. Once the water is boiling, add the pasta and cook according to the package directions, around 9 minutes. Use a spider or slotted spoon to transfer the pasta to a large bowl. Let the water return to a full boil, add the asparagus, and cook until just tender and still bright green, about 3 minutes. Pour into a colander set in the sink, and then add to the bowl of warm rigatoni.

2. While the pasta and vegetables cook, melt the butter in a medium-sized heavy saucepan over medium heat. Once the butter has melted, add the leeks and sauté until very aromatic and soft, about 6 minutes. Whisk in the flour and cook, whisking until it disappears, about 1 minute. Add the milk, half of the chives, half of the lemon zest, the remaining ½ teaspoon salt, the nutmeg, and pepper, and simmer, whisking occasionally, until thick, about 4 minutes. Add both cheeses, remove from the heat, and whisk until smooth.

3. Pour the sauce into the bowl with the pasta and asparagus. Toss well, and serve portions garnished with the remaining 2 tablespoons chives and 1 teaspoon zest.

SERVING SUGGESTIONS: Begin your meal with a tomato or baby beet salad and finish with a strawberry tart and fresh mint tea.

Lentils with Indian Spices and Coconut

SERVES 4 TO 6

Be sure to use the garnishes—they add color, brightness, and texture to this comforting South Indian-inspired vegan entrée. You can purchase pomegranate arils (seeds) already removed from the fruits in the produce section at grocery stores or frozen at some stores (such as Trader Joe's). Opt for garam masala without salt. Thick, tart tamarind concentrate is available in the Asian section of grocery stores. ¶ If you are reheating the lentils a day or so after preparing them, feel free to add more liquid (such as vegetable broth or water) to loosen them—just taste again and add more garam masala or salt, if necessary.

3 tablespoons vegetable oil, divided

1 cup finely chopped red onions

Scant 1 cup finely chopped carrots

3 tablespoons finely chopped scallions, white and light green parts only

1 tablespoon plus ½ teaspoon minced peeled fresh ginger

2 teaspoons finely chopped garlic

1½ teaspoons garam masala (without salt)

3 tablespoons tomato paste

1 pound dried brown lentils

2 cups reduced-sodium vegetable broth (not stock)

1½ teaspoons coarse salt

One 13½-ounce can light coconut milk, shaken

2 tablespoons tamarind concentrate

4 to 6 cups cooked rice or rice pilaf, for serving

1. Heat 2 tablespoons of the oil in a large, heavy Dutch oven over medium-high heat. When hot, add the onions, carrots, scallions, ginger, garlic, and garam masala, and sauté until the onions are soft, about 8 minutes.

2. Stir in the remaining 1 tablespoon oil plus the tomato paste and lentils, and cook for 2 minutes. Add the broth, 4 cups water, and the salt, and bring to a boil over high heat, stirring occasionally.

3. As soon as the mixture comes to a boil, cover the pot, reduce the heat to medium low, and simmer until the lentils are very tender, about another 30 minutes. Stir in the coconut milk and tamarind, recover, and simmer over medium-low heat for another 2 minutes (the lentils should be very tender, and the pot should include some liquid, but not so much that the mixture is very soupy).

4. Use a potato masher to mash the lentils a bit. Then ladle portions over rice, garnishing each serving with pomegranate seeds, toasted coconut, cilantro, lime wedges, and—if desired—soy yogurt.

Fresh pomegranate arils
  (seeds), for serving

Lightly toasted unsweetened
  coconut, for serving

Chopped fresh cilantro leaves,
  for serving

Lime wedges, for serving

Plain soy yogurt, for serving
  (optional)

SERVING SUGGESTIONS: Prepare a lime-coconut rice pilaf, using coconut milk and vegetable broth or water for the liquid and stirring freshly grated lime zest into the cooked rice for flavor. For dessert, try sliced fresh mango with lime wedges.

TRY THIS: Buy whole pomegranates and remove the arils yourself. Halve the pomegranate horizontally, place it in a large water-filled bowl, and pull the arils out from the white membranes. You can also thwak the backside of each half with your fist to knock out some arils.

Seaweed-Crusted Tofu with Remoulade Sauce

SERVES 4

This crunchy-on-the-outside and tender-on-the-inside pan-fried tofu stars panko for crunch and seaweed flakes and Old Bay® seasoning for that salty, at-the-shore flavor. A mild remoulade sauce alongside is the ideal creamy dipper—don't omit it (if you do, add about ⅛ teaspoon of coarse salt total when seasoning both sides of the tofu). ❡ You can find Dulse seaweed flakes at natural food stores or Whole Foods Market. If you'd like your remoulade to be spicy, add some minced jalapeños. To make the entrée vegan, use a vegan mayonnaise and an egg substitute, and substitute another tablespoon of oil for the butter when pan-frying.

One 14-ounce package extra-firm tofu

½ cup mayonnaise

¼ cup finely chopped shallots

¼ packed cup fresh flat-leaf parsley leaves

8 cornichons, chopped

1 tablespoon plus 1 teaspoon ketchup

2 teaspoons fresh-squeezed, strained lemon juice

1 teaspoon Dijon mustard

½ teaspoon lemon zest

¼ plus ⅛ teaspoon coarse salt

⅓ cup unbleached all-purpose flour

2 large eggs

1 cup panko breadcrumbs

1 tablespoon Dulse seaweed flakes

1. Overlap three paper towels on a plate. Top with the tofu, then another three overlapping paper towels, and another plate. Let sit for 30 minutes.

2. While the tofu drains, add the mayonnaise, shallots, parsley, cornichons, ketchup, lemon juice, mustard, zest, and salt to a food processor and purée until smooth, about 20 seconds (you should yield 1 cup). Set aside.

3. Pour the flour into a medium-sized bowl. To a second medium-sized bowl, add the eggs and 2 tablespoons water, and whisk well until smooth. In a large bowl, stir together the panko, Dulse, and ½ teaspoon of the Old Bay seasoning. Once the tofu has drained, cut it widthwise into 8 slices (all the same size). Line up the tofu slices, then sprinkle both sides evenly with the remaining ¼ teaspoon Old Bay seasoning; rub it into the tofu.

4. One slice at a time, dredge the tofu in the flour to coat both sides, shaking off any excess; then the egg mixture to coat both sides, shaking off any excess; then the panko mixture to coat both sides, shaking off any excess.

¾ teaspoon Old Bay seasoning,
divided

¼ cup plus 1 tablespoon
vegetable oil, divided

1 tablespoon unsalted butter

4 lemon wedges, for serving

5. Once the tofu slices have been breaded, add 3 tablespoons oil and the butter to a 10-inch, heavy, nonstick sauté pan, and heat over medium high. Once the butter has melted and the pan is hot, add half of the breaded tofu slices and cook until both sides are golden brown and crisp, turning over halfway through, 6 to 7 minutes total. Transfer to a plate. Add the remaining 2 tablespoons oil and the remaining tofu slices and repeat the cooking process, about another 6 minutes.

6. Place 2 slices of tofu on each of four serving plates; arrange a lemon wedge and a small bowl of the remoulade sauce alongside. Serve immediately.

SERVING SUGGESTIONS: Pair this "seafood" dish with corn on the cob, sliced tomatoes, and blueberry pie for dessert.

TRY THIS: Make "fish" sandwiches by placing the pan-fried tofu on buns, with tomato slices and lettuce leaves. Serve with the homemade remoulade.

Spanakopita with Roasted Red Peppers

Here, roasted red peppers, fresh herbs, and lemon zest jazz up a decadent Greek standard. Plan ahead: the phyllo dough—which you should be able to find in the freezer section at your grocery store—must first be defrosted, which takes several hours. For ease, place it in the refrigerator to defrost the night before. ¶ Make sure the melted butter is not hot, and don't use part-skim ricotta—it's too watery. Once the phyllo dough has been removed from the box, work quickly so it doesn't dry out (hence, the damp kitchen towel and waxed paper for covering in Step 4).

12 sheets phyllo dough

3 tablespoons extra-virgin olive oil, divided

½ cup finely chopped red onions

½ cup thinly sliced scallions, white and light green parts only

1 tablespoon plus 1 teaspoon minced garlic

1½ pounds fresh spinach, washed, stems removed, and leaves roughly chopped

12 ounces crumbled feta

1 cup whole milk ricotta

One 10-ounce jar roasted red peppers, drained and chopped, then drained again

¼ cup plus 1 tablespoon chopped fresh flat-leaf parsley leaves

continued

1. Remove the defrosted phyllo dough (still in the box) from the fridge and let it sit at room temperature for 2 hours. Meanwhile, heat 2 tablespoons oil in a 12-inch, heavy, nonstick frying pan over medium-high heat. When hot, add the onions, scallions, and garlic, and sauté until softened, about 3 minutes. Add the spinach one handful at a time, tossing with tongs to wilt; continue adding and cooking the spinach until all of it is very tender and some of the liquid has evaporated, about 7 minutes. Remove from the heat.

2. Transfer the spinach mixture to a cutting board and chop, then add to a large bowl lined with a clean kitchen towel. Let the mixture sit until it's cool enough to handle, then form a bundle with the kitchen towel and squeeze the spinach to thoroughly drain.

3. Pour out any spinach liquid from the bowl. Add the drained spinach plus the feta, ricotta, roasted red peppers, parsley, dill, lemon zest, salt, pepper, and nutmeg. Mix very well with tongs or your hands. Cover with plastic wrap and chill until the phyllo has sat out for 2 hours. Heat the oven to 350°F.

continued

¼ **cup plus 1 tablespoon
chopped fresh dill**

1 heaping teaspoon lemon zest

¼ **teaspoon coarse salt**

8 grinds black pepper

¼ **teaspoon ground nutmeg**

**8 tablespoons (1 stick) unsalted
butter, melted**

4. When ready to assemble and bake the dish, place the bowl of filling, a 9 x 13 x 2-inch baking dish, the melted butter, a pastry brush, and the remaining 1 tablespoon olive oil on the counter. Using the pastry brush, brush the entire interior of the baking dish with a bit of the butter to grease it. Place a baking sheet on the counter next to the ingredients; carefully place the phyllo sheets on it and cover them with a sheet of waxed paper and a damp, clean kitchen towel.

5. Gently place 1 sheet of phyllo in the baking dish, folding over the sides to make it fit. Brush with some of the melted butter. Place another phyllo sheet on top and brush with more melted butter. Repeat four more times. Spoon the filling on top and spread evenly. Cover with another sheet of phyllo dough and brush with more butter. Repeat five more times. Score the top of the final phyllo sheet gently into serving shapes, without puncturing the filling. Brush the top with the remaining tablespoon of oil. Place in the oven and bake until golden brown on top and flaky, about 45 minutes. Cut and serve.

SERVING SUGGESTIONS: Serve with a Greek salad, with baklava for dessert.

TRY THIS: Spanakopita is a classic appetizer for parties. This version will take less time to make than individual spanakopita triangles, since it's cooked in a large baking dish. To serve as a starter, simply score the phyllo before baking into smaller servings instead of in large dinner-sized portions.

Whole Wheat Spaghetti with White Bean Balls

SERVES 4

Mashed white beans sub in for ground meat in these tender, golden-brown faux meatballs served atop whole wheat spaghetti dressed with fresh tomato sauce. Adults and kids alike will love them. The recipe makes about 4 cups of sauce; you'll use about half and have 2 cups left over for the week (or to freeze).

About ½ cup extra-virgin olive oil, divided

2 tablespoons plus 1 teaspoon minced garlic, divided

⅛ teaspoon crushed red pepper flakes

Two 24-ounce cans strained unsalted tomatoes, such as Muir Glen

6 sprigs fresh oregano, tied together with kitchen twine and ½ teaspoon minced fresh oregano leaves, divided

2 teaspoons coarse salt, plus extra for salting the pasta water, divided

15 grinds black pepper, divided

½ cup finely chopped red onions

½ cup finely chopped fennel

Two large slices white country bread

⅓ cup plus 3 tablespoons 2% milk

One 15-ounce can white beans, rinsed and drained

continued

1. Heat 1 tablespoon oil in a medium-sized, heavy saucepan with high sides over medium heat. When hot, add 2 tablespoons minced garlic and the red pepper flakes and sauté until aromatic, no more than 1 minute. Immediately add the tomatoes, oregano sprigs, 1 teaspoon salt, and 5 grinds pepper. Raise the heat to medium high and simmer until the sauce is thick and reduced by about a third, about 30 minutes (you should yield about 4 cups of sauce). Carefully remove and discard the oregano. Turn off the heat.

2. Heat another tablespoon of the oil in a 12-inch, heavy, nonstick sauté pan over medium-high heat. When hot, add the red onions, fennel, and the remaining 1 teaspoon minced garlic, and sauté until soft, aromatic, and slightly golden brown, about 5 minutes. Set aside off the heat to cool a bit.

3. Meanwhile, add the bread and milk to a medium-sized bowl. Squeeze together with your hands until you form a paste. Add the drained beans, ½ cup cheese, the minced oregano, sage, rosemary, egg, the remaining 1 teaspoon salt, and the remaining 10 grinds pepper. Stir in the sautéed onion-fennel mixture. Use a potato masher to mash the mixture very well, then grab a bit with your hands (it will feel wet and a bit sticky) and shape into 16 balls.

4. Wipe out the sauté pan to clean it. Heat 3 tablespoons oil over medium-high heat. When hot, add 8 bean balls and cook until they're crisp and golden brown on all sides, turning over halfway through, about 9 minutes total. Transfer to a plate and repeat with the remaining bean balls and another 3 tablespoons or so of oil, about another 9 minutes.

continued

¾ cup freshly grated
Parmigiano-Reggiano, divided

½ teaspoon minced fresh sage
leaves

½ teaspoon minced fresh
rosemary sprigs

1 large egg, beaten

8 ounces whole wheat spaghetti

5. While the bean balls are cooking, cook the spaghetti. Fill a medium-sized heavy saucepan two-thirds full of heavily salted water, cover, and bring to a boil over high heat. Once the water comes to a boil, add the spaghetti, and cook until al dente, stirring occasionally, 7 to 8 minutes (follow the package directions). Once the pasta has finished cooking, drain in a colander set in the sink.

6. Pour the drained spaghetti back into the hot, empty saucepan (in which you cooked it). Add 2 cups of the sauce and toss with tongs. Divide the dressed spaghetti between four large, shallow soup bowls; top each serving with 4 bean balls. Garnish each portion with the remaining ¼ cup of cheese. Serve with additional sauce at the table, if desired.

SERVING SUGGESTIONS: Serve a salad (perhaps frisée with orange, red onions, and fennel) alongside. Finish the meal with brownie sundaes.

TRY THIS: Fennel can hold a lot of dirt. The best way to wash it is to first cut the bulb from the fronds, then cut the bulb in half, core, and slice, leaving you with large half-moons. Put those in a bowl of cold water and swish around with your fingers. Remove the fennel from the water, discard the dirty water, and rinse one more time to ensure the dirt is gone.

Veggie Burgers with Brown Rice, Fresh Parsley, and Chickpeas

SERVES 6

Chockful of flavorful, healthful ingredients (brown rice, mushrooms, carrots, onions, parsley, garlic, and chickpeas), these vegan burgers are sure to become a weeknight and company staple. Cook the brown rice ahead of time or use rice left over from another meal. Vary the recipe by substituting pinto beans for the chickpeas and omit the cheese if you like.

¼ cup uncooked short-grain brown rice

½ teaspoon coarse salt, plus extra for cooking the rice, divided

¼ cup plus 1 tablespoon vegetable oil, divided

1 tablespoon coarsely chopped garlic

1 large portabella mushroom cap, coarsely chopped

One 15-ounce can chickpeas, rinsed and drained

½ cup shredded carrots

Heaping ¼ cup fresh flat-leaf parsley leaves

¼ cup ketchup, plus additional for serving, if desired

¼ packed cup coarsely chopped red onions

2 tablespoons Dijon mustard, plus additional for serving, if desired

continued

1. Fill a small- to medium-sized saucepan two-thirds full of heavily salted water, cover, and bring to a boil over high heat. Once the water is boiling, stir in the rice and cook, stirring occasionally, until tender, about 40 minutes. Pour into a colander set in the sink and let cool to room temperature, about 15 minutes (the rice should have doubled in volume, to a bit more than ½ cup).

2. Meanwhile, heat 1 tablespoon oil in a small, heavy, nonstick sauté pan over medium-high heat. When hot, add the garlic and sauté until slightly softened, 1 to 2 minutes (watch carefully to prevent burning). Immediately add the mushrooms and sauté, stirring, until tender and browned, about 5 minutes. Set aside off the heat to cool (you should yield ½ cup).

3. Add the cooked rice, the garlic-mushroom mixture, ¼ teaspoon salt, the chickpeas, carrots, parsley, ketchup, onions, mustard, soy sauce, chipotle liquid, and black pepper to the bowl of a food processor. Purée until the burger mixture is combined well, about 40 seconds.

4. Mix the panko and the remaining ¼ teaspoon salt in a large bowl. Add the burger mixture and mix well with your hands until combined. Shape into 6 patties and flatten each one to about ½ inch thick, using your fingers to make an indentation in the center of each.

continued

1 tablespoon reduced-sodium
  soy sauce

1 teaspoon liquid from canned
  chipotles en adobo

8 grinds black pepper

1 cup panko breadcrumbs

6 thin slices soy cheese

6 brioche buns, split and toasted

6 tomato slices, drained on a
  paper towel

2 ripe avocados, thinly sliced

½ cup bean or radish sprouts,
  washed and dried

5. Heat 2 tablespoons oil in a 10-inch, heavy, nonstick sauté pan over medium-high heat. When the oil is hot, add 4 patties and cook until the first side is browned, about 3 minutes. Flip over and cover each patty with a slice of cheese. Cover the pan and reduce the heat to medium. Continue cooking until the cheese has melted and the other side is browned, about another 3 minutes. Transfer to a plate. Raise the heat to medium high, and add the remaining 2 tablespoons of oil and remaining 2 patties to the pan. Repeat the cooking process, turning the burgers over after about 3 minutes, then adding the cheese, covering the pan, reducing the heat to medium, and cooking until the cheese has melted.

6. Place a patty on half of each bun and top with a tomato slice, some avocado slices, and some sprouts. Serve immediately, passing ketchup and mustard at the table.

SERVING SUGGESTIONS: Serve these vegan burgers—true all-American comfort food—with pickles and fries on the side and a sundae for dessert.

Stuffed Acorn Squash with Chickpeas and Moroccan Spices

SERVES 4

This gorgeous, sweet-and-spicy vegan dish makes an impressive holiday entrée (double the recipe to feed a large crowd). Although it looks impressive, it's actually fairly quick and easy to prepare.

¼ cup plus 3 tablespoons extra-virgin olive oil, divided

2 acorn squash (each one about 1 pound 7 ounces), halved widthwise

2 teaspoons dark brown sugar, divided

1 teaspoon ground cumin, divided

¾ teaspoon ground cinnamon, divided

1 teaspoon coarse salt, divided

¼ teaspoon ground cayenne, divided

14 grinds black pepper, divided

1 cup finely chopped red onions

1 cup finely chopped carrots

1 cup finely chopped red bell peppers

1 tablespoon finely chopped garlic

1 tablespoon finely chopped peeled fresh ginger

½ teaspoon ground coriander

One 15-ounce can chickpeas, rinsed and drained

continued

1. Heat the oven to 400°F. Grease a large (9 x 13 x 2 inches) glass baking dish with 1 tablespoon oil. Place the 4 squash halves cut side up in the baking dish (despite the stems on two halves, they should lie flat). Sprinkle the squash evenly with a total of 1 teaspoon sugar, ½ teaspoon cumin, ¼ teaspoon cinnamon, ¼ teaspoon salt, ⅛ teaspoon cayenne, and 8 grinds black pepper. Drizzle evenly with 2 tablespoons oil. Bake, uncovered, until tender and golden brown, about 50 minutes.

2. Meanwhile, heat 2 tablespoons oil in a heavy medium-sized saucepan over medium-high heat. When hot, add the onions, carrots, bell peppers, garlic, ginger, 1 teaspoon sugar, ½ teaspoon cumin, ½ teaspoon cinnamon, ½ teaspoon coriander, ½ teaspoon salt, ⅛ teaspoon cayenne, and 6 grinds black pepper. Sauté until the vegetables are tender, about 7 minutes. Add the chickpeas, tomatoes, currants, and lemon juice, and simmer for 6 minutes. Remove from the heat.

3. While the vegetables cook, heat 2 tablespoons oil in a small, heavy, nonstick sauté pan over medium-high heat. When hot, add the panko and ¼ teaspoon salt, and cook, stirring, until the breadcrumbs are very lightly golden brown, about 3 minutes. Immediately remove from the heat and set aside.

continued

¼ cup plus 2 tablespoons
strained, canned tomatoes,
such as Muir Glen

¼ cup currants

2 tablespoons freshly squeezed,
strained lemon juice

⅓ cup panko breadcrumbs

¼ cup finely chopped fresh
cilantro leaves, divided

1 cup plain soy yogurt, for
serving (optional)

4. When the squash comes out of the oven, divide the chickpea filling evenly among the squash cavities. Pack it down (it will overflow a bit) and cover the baking dish with aluminum foil. Return the pan to the oven and bake until the squash is very tender and the filling is hot, about another 20 minutes.

5. Sprinkle each serving with one-quarter of the cilantro and one-quarter of the breadcrumbs. Serve with the soy yogurt, if desired.

SERVING SUGGESTIONS: Serve this nourishing show-stopper with braised greens and couscous (follow the package instructions for four servings, and stir in about 12 chopped pitted olives, a bit of salt, some extra virgin olive oil, and a bit of freshly grated lemon zest). For dessert, offer rice pudding with cardamon and rosewater.

Polenta Lasagna with Puttanesca Sauce and Herbed Ricotta

SERVES 8 TO 10

This satisfying, easy-to-prepare twist on lasagna stars polenta rounds (instead of noodles) and a tomato sauce accented with salty olives and capers. You should end up with an extra cup of sauce—serve alongside the lasagna for those with a yen for a bit more.

2 tablespoons extra-virgin olive oil, divided

2 tablespoons minced garlic

⅛ teaspoon crushed red pepper flakes

Two 28-ounce cans strained unsalted tomatoes, such as Muir Glen

1 cup coarsely chopped rinsed and drained pitted Kalamata olives

One 2.4-oz. jar rinsed, drained nonpareil capers

6 sprigs fresh oregano, tied together with kitchen twine

Two 18-ounce tubes precooked polenta, sliced into ½-inch-thick rounds (about 24 rounds)

1½ teaspoons coarse salt, divided

20 grinds black pepper, divided

One 32-ounce container whole milk ricotta cheese, strained over a colander to remove excess liquid

1 cup freshly grated Parmigiano-Reggiano, divided

continued

1. Heat the oven to 375°F. Heat 1 tablespoon oil in a medium-sized, heavy saucepan with high sides over medium heat. When hot, add the garlic and red pepper flakes and sauté until aromatic, no more than 1 minute. Immediately add the tomatoes, olives, capers, and oregano; raise the heat to medium high and simmer until thick and reduced by about a third, about 30 minutes (you should yield 4 cups of sauce). Carefully remove and discard the oregano and set the sauce aside off the heat.

2. Lay the polenta rounds on a large surface and season both sides evenly with a total of 1 teaspoon salt and 12 grinds pepper. In a medium-sized bowl, stir together the ricotta, half of the Parmigiano-Reggiano, the parsley, eggs, remaining ½ teaspoon salt, and remaining 8 grinds pepper. Whisk very well to combine (no yolk should be visible).

3. Grease the inside of a 9 x 13 x 2-inch (3-quart) baking dish with the remaining 1 tablespoon oil; place the baking dish on a baking sheet with sides. Ladle 1 cup of sauce into the bottom of the dish and spread it around a bit. Top with half of the polenta, arranging it evenly. Spread evenly with half of the ricotta mixture. Ladle another cup of sauce on top, then evenly arrange the remaining polenta rounds on top. Spread the remaining ricotta mixture evenly on top. Ladle on another cup of sauce, then arrange the sliced mozzarella on top and sprinkle with the remaining ½ cup Parmigiano-Reggiano.

continued

¼ cup finely chopped fresh
  flat-leaf parsley leaves

2 large eggs

1 pound fresh mozzarella
  cheese, wiped dry with a clean
  towel and sliced thin

4. Bake, uncovered, until the cheese on top completely melts and
is golden brown in a few spots, and the sauce thickens and
bubbles, about 40 minutes. Let sit for at least 30 minutes
(to allow the lasagna to set), and then serve.

SERVING SUGGESTIONS: Begin your meal with an endive
and radicchio salad with oranges and a balsamic
dressing. Finish with red wine–poached pears served
with chocolate sauce.

TRY THIS: Feel free to use cooked lasagna noodles instead
of the polenta rounds. If you prefer tomato sauce on the
plainer side, omit the olives and capers.

Four-Cheese Mac and Cheese with Smoked Paprika and Garlic-Thyme Breadcrumbs

SERVES 8

The whole wheat pasta shells in this oozy and cheesy Spanish-inspired mac and cheese temper the richness a bit.

8 tablespoons (1 stick) unsalted butter, at room temperature, divided

1¾ teaspoons coarse salt, plus extra for salting the pasta water, divided

1 pound whole wheat pasta shells

¼ cup unbleached all-purpose flour

3 cups 2% milk

½ teaspoon pimentón de la Vera dulce (sweet Spanish smoked paprika)

15 grinds black pepper, divided

2 tablespoons Dijon mustard

1¼ packed cups grated Gruyère

1¼ packed cups grated Manchego

1 cup grated mild Cheddar

¼ packed cup grated Parmigiano-Reggiano

One 12-ounce jar grilled piquillo peppers in water, drained and coarsely chopped

½ cup panko breadcrumbs

2 teaspoons minced garlic

1½ teaspoons minced fresh thyme leaves

1. Heat the oven to 375°F, and grease a 9 x 13 x 2-inch glass baking dish with a scant 1 tablespoon butter. Fill a medium-sized saucepan two-thirds full of heavily salted water, cover, and bring to a boil. Once boiling, stir in the pasta and cook, stirring occasionally, for 14 to 15 minutes (follow the package directions). Drain the pasta in a colander set in the sink.

2. While the pasta cooks, melt 6 tablespoons butter in a medium-sized, heavy saucepan over medium heat. Once melted, whisk in the flour; keep whisking until a pale yellow, smooth, bubbly sauce forms, about 1 minute. Raise the heat to medium high. Immediately add the milk, 1½ teaspoons salt, the pimentón, and 10 grinds pepper; keep simmering, whisking frequently, until the mixture becomes thick and smooth and just begins to form larger bubbles, about 7 minutes.

3. Reduce the heat to medium low, and whisk in the mustard and cheeses. When smooth, remove from the heat, and whisk in the chopped piquillo peppers until very smooth. Add the pasta to the sauce, mix well, and spoon in the baking dish.

4. Melt the remaining 1 tablespoon butter in a medium microwave-safe bowl in the microwave. Once melted, stir in the breadcrumbs, garlic, thyme, the remaining ¼ teaspoon salt, and the remaining 5 grinds pepper. Stir very well. Evenly sprinkle the topping over the mac and cheese.

5. Transfer to the oven and bake until the sauce is bubbly and the topping is crisp, about 40 minutes. Serve.

SERVING SUGGESTIONS: Serve this with a light frisée and tomato salad, with chocolate-covered baguette slices (drizzled with olive oil and sprinkled with sea salt).

Pizza with Zucchini and Smoked Mozzarella

SERVES 4

Sautéed zucchini and smoked mozzarella stand in for pepperoni in this crowd-pleasing entrée. Raw garlic in the uncooked, ready-in-10-minutes tomato sauce adds punch. If you don't want to wait the hour for the dough to become easier to work with, use a store-bought ready-to-heat flatbread crust and follow the package instructions. For heat-lovers, drizzle the finished pie with chile oil.

About ¼ cup plus 1 tablespoon extra-virgin olive oil, divided

20 ounces refrigerated or frozen and thawed pizza dough, white or whole wheat

1 large zucchini, trimmed and thinly sliced on the bias

¼ teaspoon ground fennel seed

¼ teaspoon dried oregano

¾ teaspoon coarse salt, divided

⅛ teaspoon crushed red pepper flakes

9 grinds black pepper, divided

¼ cup plus 1 tablespoon tomato paste

¾ cup plus 2 tablespoons strained canned tomatoes, such as Muir Glen

½ tablespoon finely chopped garlic

1 tablespoon finely chopped fresh oregano leaves

1 pound smoked mozzarella, thinly sliced

Chile oil, for drizzling (optional)

1. Very lightly oil the inside of a medium-sized bowl with about ½ tablespoon oil, then place the dough ball inside it. Cover with a dishtowel and let sit for 1 to 2 hours.

2. Meanwhile, heat 2 tablespoons oil in a 10-inch, heavy, non-stick sauté pan, and heat over medium high. When hot, add the zucchini slices, fennel, dried oregano, ¼ teaspoon salt, the red pepper flakes, and 4 grinds pepper; sauté until tender, about 6 minutes, then set aside off the heat.

3. To make the sauce, add the tomato paste, strained tomatoes, garlic, fresh oregano, ½ teaspoon salt, 5 grinds pepper, and 2 tablespoons olive oil to the bowl of a food processor or a blender. Purée until smooth, about 30 seconds. (You should yield about 1¼ cups sauce.)

4. Heat the oven to 500°F. Lightly grease a baking sheet with ½ tablespoon oil. Place the dough on top and use your fingers to stretch it into a 16-inch round or large rectangle. Pour the remaining oil from the bowl on top and spread it over the dough with your fingers. Spread sauce evenly on top of the dough, leaving a ½-inch border on all sides (if you prefer your pizza saucy, use all of the sauce). Top evenly with the mozzarella and zucchini. Bake until the cheese melts and the dough is cooked through, about 10 minutes. Serve, drizzled with chile oil, if desired.

SERVING SUGGESTIONS: Offer garden salad or sautéed corn alongside and sliced peaches with zabaglione for dessert.

Mushroom-Vegetable Loaf

SERVES 6

A vegetarian take on meatloaf, this entrée is savory and satisfying thanks to mushrooms, tomato paste, and soy sauce. I like to use an 8½ x 4¼ x 3-inch loaf pan, but feel free to go with other sizes (you just might need to adjust the cooking time slightly).

¼ teaspoon coarse salt, plus more as needed

½ cup short-grain brown rice

2 tablespoons extra-virgin olive oil

20 ounces white button mushrooms, coarsely chopped

2 cups thinly sliced (⅛ inch) carrots

1 cup coarsely chopped red onions

1 cup thinly sliced celery

1 tablespoon plus 1½ teaspoons finely chopped garlic

One 6-ounce can tomato paste, such as Muir Glen

1 cup canned lentils, rinsed and drained

½ cup quick-cooking oats

½ cup finely chopped fresh flat-leaf parsley leaves

¼ cup reduced-sodium soy sauce

1 teaspoon dried oregano

10 grinds black pepper

1 large egg, beaten

⅓ cup ketchup

1 tablespoon balsamic vinegar

1. Heat the oven to 375°F. Meanwhile, fill a small- to medium-sized heavy saucepan about two-thirds full of heavily salted water, cover, and bring to a boil over high heat. Once boiling, stir in the rice and boil, stirring occasionally, until tender, 35 to 40 minutes. Drain in a colander in the sink, and let cool for a bit. Measure out 1 cup of cooked rice.

2. Heat the oil in a medium-sized, heavy Dutch oven over medium-high heat. When hot, add the mushrooms, carrots, onions, celery, and garlic, and sauté, stirring occasionally, until the mixture is slightly reduced in volume and the vegetables are beginning to soften, about 5 minutes. Stir in the tomato paste, and continue cooking until the vegetables are tender, about another 14 minutes.

3. In a medium-sized bowl, stir together the 1 cup of cooked rice, lentils, oats, parsley, soy sauce, oregano, the remaining ¼ teaspoon salt, and the black pepper. Use a potato masher to mash together, pushing down hard on the lentils to smash them a bit. Add this mixture to the cooked vegetables in the Dutch oven, stir well, and transfer to the bowl of a food processor.

4. Pulse until the mixture is relatively smooth and very well mixed, using a spatula to push the ingredients at the top down to the bottom, a minute or two. Pour back into the bowl and stir in the beaten egg, mixing well to incorporate.

5. Spray the entire interior of a loaf pan with cooking spray. Ladle the mixture into the pan and use a spatula to spread the top flat. Bake for 30 minutes. Meanwhile, in a small bowl, combine the ketchup and vinegar, mixing well. Spread this glaze evenly over the top and continue to bake the loaf until the glaze has thickened and darkened in color, about another 20 minutes. Let the loaf cool at room temperature for about 10 minutes, then slice and carefully transfer the slices to serving plates. (If you'd like the slices to be perfectly set, chill for at least an hour before serving and then microwave individual portions.)

SERVING SUGGESTIONS: Try slices alongside mashed potatoes or polenta and peas. Chocolate pudding would be the ideal comfort-food dessert.

TRY THIS: Once chilled and sliced, individual loaf servings are easily portable for brown-bag lunches. Slices can also be used as sandwich filling.

Roasted Beet "Steaks" with Red Wine–Mushroom Sauce and Rice with Chickpeas and Root Vegetables

SERVES 4

This full meal brings fancy-restaurant flavor and visual appeal to humble beets, mushrooms, and rice. Sip the remainder of the red wine you use in the sweet and earthy dish with the meal. Make sure to prepare the sauce at the last minute; keep the roasted beets and the rice pilaf covered and warm while you make it. If you don't have saffron threads, don't worry—they simply add a subtle yellow color and floral aroma to the rice.

4 small (5½ ounces each) red beets

6 tablespoons (½ stick plus 2 tablespoons) unsalted butter, divided

1 cup finely chopped red onions

1 cup finely chopped red bell peppers, seeds and membranes removed and discarded

Scant 1 cup finely chopped carrots

2 teaspoons finely chopped garlic, divided

1 cup uncooked long-grain brown rice, such as brown basmati, rinsed and drained

2½ cups reduced-sodium vegetable broth (not stock), divided

2¼ teaspoons coarse salt, divided

A few threads saffron (optional)

continued

1. Heat the oven to 400°F. When hot, wrap the beets in aluminum foil (in packages of 2 each) and roast until tender when poked with a fork, about 1 hour. (When done and out of the oven, rewrap in the foil to keep warm.)

2. Meanwhile, heat 2 tablespoons butter in a medium-sized, heavy saucepan over medium heat. When melted, add the onions, bell peppers, carrots, and half of the garlic, and sauté until the onions are completely tender, about 3 minutes. Stir in the rice, and cook for 2 minutes. Add 2 cups broth, ½ teaspoon salt, and the saffron, and bring to a boil over high heat. As soon as the liquid is boiling, cover the pot, and reduce the heat to medium low. Simmer until the rice is tender and the liquid has evaporated, about 20 minutes. Fluff the rice with a fork. Stir in the chickpeas, ½ teaspoon salt, and another tablespoon of butter; cover and set aside off the heat to steam for 5 minutes.

3. Heat 2 tablespoons butter in a 10-inch, heavy sauté pan over medium-high heat. As soon as the butter has melted, add the shallots and the remaining garlic, and sauté until softened, about 2 minutes. Add the mushrooms and sauté, stirring, for 2 minutes. Stir in the flour, and cook for 1 minute, then remove from the heat and add the wine. Return the pan to the

continued

One 15-ounce can chickpeas,
rinsed and drained

½ cup finely chopped shallots

7 ounces mushrooms (I prefer
shiitake), stems discarded and
caps thinly sliced

1 tablespoon unbleached
all-purpose flour

1 cup full-bodied red wine, such
as Cabernet or Merlot

17 grinds black pepper, divided

¼ cup finely chopped fresh
flat-leaf parsley leaves, plus
another 2 tablespoons for
garnish

heat and raise the heat to high. Cook, scraping the bottom of
the pan with a wooden spoon, until the wine reduces and the
sauce thickens, about 3 minutes. Add the remaining ½ cup
broth, ¾ teaspoon salt, and 5 grinds pepper, and continue
boiling until the sauce thickens further, another 6 to 7 minutes. Stir in the remaining 1 tablespoon butter, then set aside.

4. On a cutting board, peel the beets, then trim off their ends.
Cut each beet into 5 slices. Line up the slices and season
evenly with a total of ½ teaspoon salt and 12 grinds pepper.

5. Stir the ¼ cup fresh parsley into the rice and refluff. Ladle
a scoop of the rice pilaf onto each serving plate. Arrange
5 beet slices around it, then spoon a quarter of the sauce over
the beet slices, and garnish with a quarter of the remaining
parsley.

SERVING SUGGESTION: Begin with a goat cheese salad. Rich
dark chocolate pudding or mousse will finish off this meal
perfectly.

Classic Eggplant Parmesan

SERVES 4 TO 6

Eggplant Parmesan is a perfect dish, so it requires no gilding. You do, however, need to follow a few tips to ensure the best flavor and texture. You'll taste the oil, so go with extra-virgin. There's no need to salt and drain the eggplant, so skip that common step. You do want to peel the eggplant, though—it takes less than a minute and improves the texture of the dish. If you prefer your eggplant Parmesan extra-saucy, double the tomato sauce and serve the extra alongside for ladling on top of individual portions.

1 cup extra-virgin olive oil, divided, plus more as needed

2 tablespoons minced garlic

One 28-ounce can whole peeled tomatoes, such as Muir Glen

5 sprigs fresh oregano

2 tablespoons fresh-squeezed, strained orange juice

1¾ teaspoons coarse salt, divided

A heaping ¼ teaspoon black pepper, divided, plus more as needed

⅛ teaspoon crushed red pepper flakes

1 medium-sized eggplant (about 1⅓ pounds), peeled, trimmed, and sliced into ⅓-inch-thick rounds

1 cup unbleached all-purpose flour

3 large eggs

1½ cups panko breadcrumbs

continued

1. Heat the oven to 350°F. Heat 1 tablespoon oil in a small- to medium-sized, deep, heavy saucepan over medium heat. When the oil is hot, add the garlic and sauté until it's aromatic and softened, about 1 minute. Add the tomatoes, oregano, orange juice, ½ teaspoon salt, a pinch of pepper, and the red pepper flakes, and raise the heat to medium high. Simmer until the mixture is reduced by about a third, about 20 minutes, using a potato masher to crush the tomatoes a bit (you should yield about 2½ cups sauce). Remove and discard the oregano sprigs, and set the sauce aside.

2. Lay the eggplant rounds in one layer on a cutting board. Season both sides evenly with a total of 1 teaspoon salt and about ⅛ teaspoon pepper. Pour the flour into a medium-sized bowl. In a second medium-sized bowl, whisk the eggs well with 2 tablespoons water until smooth. In a large bowl, combine the panko, 1 cup grated Parmigiano-Reggiano, the lemon zest, ¼ teaspoon salt, and the remaining pepper. Arrange the bowls in this order: flour, eggs, and panko.

3. Using tongs, dip an eggplant round in flour to coat both sides and then shake off any excess. Transfer to the egg mixture and coat both sides, shaking off any excess. Transfer to the panko mixture and coat both sides, shaking off any excess. Set aside on a large surface. Repeat with all of the eggplant rounds.

continued

1½ cups freshly grated
Parmigiano-Reggiano, divided

1 heaping teaspoon lemon zest

1 cup shredded low-moisture
part-skim mozzarella, divided

½ pound fresh mozzarella,
dried with a paper towel and
thinly sliced

Fresh basil leaves, for garnish
(optional)

4. Line a large baking sheet or cutting board with paper towels. Heat ½ cup oil in a 12-inch, heavy, nonstick sauté pan with relatively high sides over medium-high heat. When the oil is hot but not smoking, add about 5 rounds of eggplant, and cook, turning over halfway through, until both sides are golden brown, about 6 minutes. Transfer to the paper towel–lined surface to degrease. Repeat with the remaining eggplant, in batches, using about another ¼ cup plus 2 tablespoons oil total (make sure there is always a thin layer of oil in the pan).

5. Once you've finished frying the eggplant, grease the inside of an 8 x 8-inch square baking dish with the remaining 1 tablespoon oil, and place the baking dish on a baking sheet with sides. Pour a third of the sauce (about ¾ cup) into the bottom of the dish. Add half of the eggplant rounds, laying them flat and overlapping them as needed. Sprinkle evenly with ½ cup shredded mozzarella. Ladle another third of the sauce evenly atop the cheese. Then place the remaining eggplant rounds on top, overlapping them to fit. Sprinkle with the remaining ½ cup shredded mozzarella, ladle on the remaining sauce, and then arrange the sliced fresh mozzarella on top to cover. Sprinkle the top with the remaining ½ cup grated Parmigiano-Reggiano.

6. Bake, uncovered, until all of the cheese melts and turns a light golden brown, about 35 minutes. Serve, garnishing each portion with some fresh basil.

SERVING SUGGESTIONS: Precede this rich, summery dish with arugula and fennel salad tossed with a bracing lemon vinaigrette. Finish with summer fruit salad lavished with lemon syrup (equal parts of sugar and water simmered with lemon peel).

Calzones with Mushrooms, Swiss Chard, and Ricotta

SERVES 4

These calzones feature a creamy, meaty center of sautéed mushrooms and Swiss chard, plus ricotta and Parmigiano-Reggiano. Feel free to serve them with marinara sauce for dipping. You can find pizza dough in the refrigerated or prepared foods section of most grocery stores. I keep it in my freezer and simply defrost it the night before I need to use it. Be sure to remove the stems from the Swiss chard for the ideal texture.

¼ cup plus 2 tablespoons extra-virgin olive oil, divided

1 ball fresh refrigerated pizza dough, whole wheat or white (about 20 ounces)

½ cup finely chopped red onions

1 tablespoon minced garlic

18 large white button mushrooms, sliced

6 cups roughly chopped fresh Swiss chard leaves, stems removed and discarded, washed and spun dry

1 tablespoon balsamic vinegar

1⅓ cups whole milk ricotta

½ cup grated Parmigiano-Reggiano

¼ teaspoon coarse salt

⅛ teaspoon crushed red pepper flakes

6 grinds black pepper

1 cup marinara sauce (see Step 1 on p. 167), for dipping (optional)

1. Drizzle a large bowl with about 1 tablespoon oil. Plop the ball of dough inside it. Cover with a kitchen towel, and let sit for 1 to 2 hours at room temperature.

2. Meanwhile, heat 2 tablespoons oil in a 12-inch, heavy, non-stick frying pan over medium-high heat. When hot, add the onions and garlic, and sauté until softened, about 3 minutes. Add the mushrooms and another 1 tablespoon oil and continue to sauté, stirring with a wooden spoon, until very tender and golden brown, about 6 minutes. Add the chopped chard leaves and toss with tongs; continue to cook until the vegetables are very tender and most of the liquid has evaporated, about 9 minutes. Add the balsamic vinegar and simmer for 2 minutes.

3. Use tongs to transfer the mixture to a bowl lined with a clean kitchen towel. Let sit until cool enough to handle, then gather into a bundle and squeeze very well to drain. Discard any liquid. Return the drained vegetable mixture to the bowl, refrigerate until it reaches room temperature, then stir in the two cheeses, salt, red pepper flakes, and black pepper. Mix very well. Heat the oven to 425°F.

4. Brush a baking sheet with 1 tablespoon oil. Turn out the pizza dough onto a clean surface. Use a bench scraper to cut it into four equal-sized pieces, then stretch each piece with your hands into a circle that's roughly 6 inches in diameter. Dollop a quarter of the filling mixture into the center of each circle, then fold the top part of the dough over the filling to create a half moon. Seal the edges by crimping or pressing. Transfer all four raw calzones to the greased baking sheet, and brush all four of their tops with the remaining 1 tablespoon oil.

5. Bake until the calzones puff and turn golden brown, 18 to 20 minutes. Let cool for about 5 minutes, then serve with marinara sauce on the side, if desired.

SERVING SUGGESTIONS: An endive and radicchio salad would make a delicious starter, as would tiramisu for dessert.

Tofu Milanese with Arugula, Cherry Tomatoes, and Balsamic Vinaigrette

SERVES 4

A tofu take on the Italian classic chicken milanese, this entrée will astonish you—you won't miss the chicken at all. Double the recipe, and this dish is ideal for a dinner party for eight.

1 pound extra-firm tofu, cut widthwise into ½-inch-thick slices (about 7 slices)

¼ cup finely chopped shallots (from 4 medium)

¼ cup balsamic vinegar

1 tablespoon fresh-squeezed, strained lemon juice

½ cup extra-virgin olive oil, divided

20 grinds black pepper, divided

1⅛ teaspoons coarse salt, divided

⅓ cup unbleached all-purpose flour

2 large eggs

1 cup panko breadcrumbs

½ cup freshly grated pecorino

¼ cup freshly grated Parmigiano-Reggiano

¼ cup finely chopped fresh flat-leaf parsley leaves

4 cups baby arugula leaves, washed and spun dry

2 cups halved cherry tomatoes

4 lemon wedges

1. Overlap three paper towels on a large plate. Place the tofu slices on top, cover with another three overlapping paper towels, and then cover with another large plate. Let sit for 30 minutes to drain.

2. Meanwhile, in a medium-sized bowl, whisk together the shallots, balsamic vinegar, lemon juice, ¼ cup olive oil, 5 grinds pepper, and ¼ teaspoon salt; set aside (you should yield a scant ¾ cup of vinaigrette).

3. Once the tofu has drained, place the flour in a medium-sized bowl. In a second medium-sized bowl, whisk together the eggs and 2 tablespoons water until smooth. In a third medium-sized bowl, stir together panko, pecorino, Parmigiano-Reggiano, parsley, ½ teaspoon salt, and 8 grinds pepper; mix well.

4. Season one side of the tofu slices evenly with a total of ⅛ teaspoon salt and 7 grinds pepper. Turn the tofu over and repeat with another ⅛ teaspoon salt (but no pepper). One slice at a time, dredge both sides of the tofu in the flour to coat, shaking off excess; then the egg mixture to coat, shaking off excess; then the breadcrumb mixture to coat, shaking off excess (you might have a bit of breadcrumb mixture left over). Transfer the breaded slices to a plate.

5. Heat the remaining ¼ cup oil in a 12-inch, heavy, nonstick sauté pan over medium-high heat. When the oil is hot, add half of the tofu and cook until crisp and golden brown on the first side, about 4 minutes; gently flip and cook the second

continued

side until it is similarly golden brown and crisp, about another 4 minutes. Transfer the slices to a paper towel–lined large plate to drain. Repeat with the remaining tofu, cooking for about another 8 minutes.

6. While the tofu is cooking, transfer the arugula and tomatoes to a large bowl. Add the remaining ⅛ teaspoon salt and 8 grinds pepper, as well as ¼ cup of the dressing. Toss well with tongs. Divide the salad between four serving plates. Onto each plate, add 1 or 2 slices of the pan-fried tofu, as well as a lemon wedge. Drizzle each serving of tofu with about 1 tablespoon of the remaining dressing, and serve.

SERVING SUGGESTIONS: Since this dish is a salad and entrée in one, all you'll need alongside it is some warm bread, with some tiramisu or a berry tart with vanilla gelato for dessert.

Indian-Spiced Lentil Patties with Mango Chutney

SERVES 4

For variety, substitute naan (Indian flatbread) for the burger buns or serve the patties over rice. Purchase a high-quality blend of garam masala. My favorite contains cumin, pepper, cinnamon, cardamom, cloves, and mace. If you don't like cilantro, try flat-leaf parsley.

One 15-ounce can lentils, drained and rinsed

1 cup panko breadcrumbs

½ cup shredded carrots

¼ cup chopped red onions

¼ cup ketchup

¼ cup fresh cilantro leaves

2 tablespoons shredded unsweetened coconut

¾ plus ⅛ teaspoon coarse salt, divided

½ teaspoon garam masala

½ teaspoon minced jalapeños (seeds and membranes removed)

10 grinds black pepper

2 tablespoons vegetable oil

1 large tomato, cored and thinly sliced

Four hamburger buns, split and toasted

¼ cup high-quality store-bought mango chutney, such as Geeta's

1 cup baby arugula leaves, washed and spun dry

1. Add the lentils, panko, carrots, onions, ketchup, cilantro, coconut, ¾ teaspoon salt, the garam masala, jalapeños, and black pepper to the bowl of a food processor. Purée until the mixture comes together, about 20 seconds. Transfer to a bowl and knead a bit, then use your hands to form four ½-inch-thick patties. Use your fingers to indent each one a bit in the center.

2. Heat the oil in a 10-inch, heavy, nonstick sauté pan over medium-high heat. When hot, add the patties and cook until golden brown on both sides, turning over and adding the remaining oil about halfway through, 7 to 8 minutes total.

3. Meanwhile, sprinkle the tomato slices evenly with the remaining ⅛ teaspoon salt. Place a patty on half of each bun. Top with about 1 tablespoon of the chutney, a seasoned tomato slice, and about ¼ cup of the arugula leaves. Serve immediately.

SERVING SUGGESTIONS: Inspired by the Indian lentil dish dal, these patties would pair well with a chickpea, tomato, chopped lettuce, and red onion salad and oven-roasted fries with cumin and mustard seed. Offer fresh mango with coconut sorbet for dessert.

Beet Wellington with Pinot Noir Sauce

SERVES 6

Here's a vegetarian twist on a classic, upscale Continental dish (which normally includes filet mignon, pâté, and truffles); but this version is inexpensive, easy (if somewhat time-consuming) to prepare, and meat-free. Rich red wine, earthy mushrooms, creamy herb-flecked goat cheese, sweet roasted beets, and flaky buttery crust meld in a harmonious, luxurious whole ideal for holidays and even weeknights. A velvety Pinot Noir sauce tops it off (though if you're time-pressed, the dish is delicious without it).

1 pound 2 ounces beets

2¼ teaspoons coarse salt, divided, plus more as needed

Scant ½ teaspoon black pepper, divided, plus more as needed

8 tablespoons (1 stick) unsalted butter, divided

⅓ cup finely chopped shallots

2 pounds cremini mushrooms, stems discarded and caps finely chopped

8 sprigs fresh thyme, tied together with kitchen twine

2¼ cups Pinot Noir or red Burgundy wine, divided

8 ounces fresh goat cheese, at room temperature

¼ cup minced fresh chives, plus another 2 tablespoons for garnish, divided

1 heaping teaspoon lemon zest

continued

1. Heat the oven to 400°F. Wrap the beets in aluminum foil and roast until they're just barely cooked through, about 50 minutes (you should be able to poke a fork in about ½ inch with some resistance). Reduce the oven temperature to 375°F.

2. When the beets are at room temperature, trim off their ends, peel, and slice into ½-inch-thick rounds (you should yield about 6 slices). Lay the slices on a large surface and season both sides evenly with a total of about a scant ½ teaspoon salt and a pinch of pepper.

3. Meanwhile, melt 3 tablespoons butter in a 12-inch, heavy, nonstick frying pan over medium-high heat. When melted, add the shallots and sauté until translucent and aromatic, about 3 minutes. Add the mushrooms, thyme, 1 teaspoon salt, and a large pinch of pepper, and sauté until the mushrooms are tender and all of the liquid has evaporated, about 13 minutes. Add ¼ cup wine and simmer until all of the liquid has evaporated, about another 7 minutes. Remove and discard the thyme sprigs, and set the mushrooms aside off the heat to cool to room temperature (you can freeze them for about 15 minutes to expedite this process). Meanwhile, mix the soft goat cheese with the ¼ cup chives, the zest, ¼ teaspoon salt, and a large pinch of pepper.

continued

About 2 tablespoons unbleached all-purpose flour for working with the puff pastry dough, divided

One 14-ounce package frozen puff pastry dough, such as Dufour, thawed

1 large egg beaten with 1 teaspoon water for egg wash

¼ cup dried wild mushrooms, enclosed in a cheesecloth bag with kitchen twine

1 tablespoon arrowroot dissolved in 1 tablespoon plus 1 teaspoon cold water

1 cup reduced-sodium vegetable broth

1 tablespoon granulated sugar or honey

4. Sprinkle about half of the flour on a large clean work surface. Unfold the puff pastry onto the surface and evenly and lightly flour both sides. Carefully stretch it a bit so it measures 12½ x 12½ inches square. Working about 5 inches down the center of the dough rectangle (leave about 3 inches each at the top and bottom and roughly 4 inches each at both sides), evenly arrange half of the mushroom mixture, then the beet slices, then the cheese mixture, and then the remaining mushroom mixture. Fold both ends of the dough over the edges of the vegetables to cover. Then fold both sides of the dough toward the center to enclose the filling completely; shape into an even rectangle. Carefully transfer the filled pastry to a parchment paper–lined baking sheet with sides. Brush the top and sides of the pastry with the egg wash. Refrigerate for 45 minutes to 2 hours.

5. Bake in the center of the 375°F oven until the pastry is golden brown, puffed, and completely firm when poked, about 50 minutes. Let sit until you've made the sauce.

6. Pour the remaining 2 cups wine into a small, heavy saucepan; place the dried mushroom sack into the wine and cook over high heat until the liquid is reduced by about half, about 16 minutes. Remove and discard the mushroom sack. Stir in the arrowroot-water mixture, the broth, sugar, the remaining ½ teaspoon salt, and the remaining pepper; lower the heat to medium and simmer (do not boil) until thickened, about 6 minutes. Whisk in the remaining 5 tablespoons butter. Taste and adjust the seasonings if necessary (you should yield about 2 cups sauce).

7. Slice the Wellington, carefully transfer to a serving platter, and garnish with the remaining chives. Serve the sauce in a gravy boat alongside the pastry or spoon some atop each serving.

SERVING SUGGESTIONS: For holidays, consider doubling the recipe by preparing two Wellingtons. Serve a frisée and apple salad alongside, with chocolate mousse for dessert.

TRY THIS:

- Plan ahead by defrosting your puff pastry; it takes 2 to 3 hours in the fridge or 1 hour at room temperature. Prepare the mushroom and goat cheese fillings and roasted beets a day ahead of time.
- When working with beets, wear plastic gloves and an apron to prevent staining.
- Use a food processor to chop the mushroom caps quickly.
- If you don't like goat cheese, substitute boursin cheese for the seasoned goat cheese-zest-chive mixture.
- Important: Don't overcook the beets; make sure the fillings are dry and at room temperature or cold prior to filling the pastry; and chill the pastry after filling.

Potato and White Bean Pie with Caramelized Onions

SERVES 6 TO 8

This is a stick-to-your-ribs, macaroni-and-cheese-like dish that's perfect for weeknights or large gatherings (kids and adults will love it). Use a trans-fat-free margarine and soy cheese to make it vegan. Save the potato skins; they make a delicious, healthful snack.

4 russet potatoes

3 tablespoons unsalted butter

1 large sweet onion, such as Vidalia, finely chopped

¼ cup plus 2 tablespoons extra-virgin olive oil, divided

1 packed tablespoon minced garlic

1 cup plain breadcrumbs

1½ plus ⅛ teaspoons coarse salt, divided

12 grinds black pepper, divided

Two 15-ounce cans white beans, rinsed and drained

2 cups 2% milk, warmed

1 packed cup grated Asiago fresco

3 tablespoons finely chopped fresh flat-leaf parsley leaves

1 teaspoon lemon zest

1. Heat the oven to 400°F. Poke the potatoes all over with the tip of a knife, then microwave until very tender and cooked through (the time will vary depending on your microwave; it takes my slow appliance 20 to 25 minutes). Alternatively, bake in the oven for about an hour. Test for tenderness by poking with a fork.

2. While the potatoes cook, heat the butter in a 10-inch, heavy sauté pan over medium heat. Once the butter has melted, add the onions and cook until they're a deep golden brown color and very tender, about 28 minutes. Set aside off of the heat.

3. Heat 2 tablespoons oil in a 10-inch, heavy sauté pan over medium-high heat. When hot, add the garlic and sauté until aromatic, no more than 1 minute (to prevent burning). Add the breadcrumbs, ⅛ teaspoon salt, and 4 grinds pepper, and cook, stirring, until golden brown, 3 or 4 minutes. Remove from the heat and pour into a bowl; set aside.

4. Once the potatoes are cool enough to handle (but still warm), cut in half with a knife and use a large spoon to scoop out the flesh. Transfer 5 packed cups of cooked potato flesh to a large bowl (reserve the remaining flesh for another use). Add the caramelized onions, drained beans, warm milk, cheese, parsley, lemon zest, and the remaining 1½ teaspoons salt and 8 grinds pepper to the potato flesh. Use a potato masher to mash a bit and then a large spoon to mix well.

5. Grease the entire inside surface of a 9 x 13 x 2-inch glass baking dish with cooking spray and dollop in the potato mixture. Spread evenly and flatten out the surface. Drizzle the top evenly with the remaining ¼ cup olive oil. Transfer to the oven and bake until the edges are a bit crispy and the top and sides are golden brown, about 45 minutes. Sprinkle the top evenly with the reserved breadcrumbs, and serve.

SERVING SUGGESTIONS: Accompany this casserole with sour cream and a side of sautéed Swiss chard and oranges. Try red wine–poached pears for dessert.

TRY THIS: Even though this dish comes together very quickly for weeknight meals, you can make it ahead. Work through Step 4, then grease the baking dish and transfer the potato mixture to it. Spread it out to flatten. Refrigerate and when ready to bake, drizzle with oil and transfer it to the oven. If the potato mixture is still cold before baking, keep it in the oven a bit longer than called for in the recipe.

Butternut Squash and Swiss Chard Stew Topped with Puff Pastry

SERVES 4 TO 6; MAKES 10 TO 12 CUPS OF STEW

Similar to potpie, this colorful, aromatic, and healthful stew is incredibly satisfying (with your eyes closed, you'd be hard-pressed to pinpoint the absence of meat). Plan ahead; the puff pastry needs to be thawed (which takes 1 to 2 hours at room temperature or 2 to 3 hours in the fridge). If you'd like to make more pastry circles, purchase two packages of puff pastry. To refashion the dish as vegan, simply omit the puff pastry and instead serve your stew with a loaf of whole-grain country bread. If you're watching your fat and calories, omit the pastry and top the stew with a dollop of Greek yogurt.

2 tablespoons extra-virgin olive oil

1 cup finely chopped fennel

1 cup finely chopped carrots

1 cup finely chopped red onions

Scant 2 tablespoons finely chopped garlic

¼ teaspoon crushed red pepper flakes

1½ teaspoons coarse salt, divided

13 grinds black pepper, divided

4 cups ½-inch cubes peeled butternut squash

3 tablespoons tomato paste

One 28-ounce can plain whole peeled tomatoes (with juices) such as Muir Glen

3½ cups reduced-sodium vegetable stock

continued

1. Heat the oven to 375°F. Heat the oil in a large, heavy saucepan or Dutch oven over medium. When hot, add the fennel, carrots, onions, garlic, red pepper flakes, ½ teaspoon salt, and 5 grinds pepper. Stir, cover the pot, and cook until the vegetables become soft and aromatic, about 8 minutes. Add the squash and tomato paste, stir, cover, and let cook for another 10 minutes (watch to make sure the squash doesn't burn). Uncover and add the tomatoes with their juices, the stock, lentils, lemon juice, and the remaining 1 teaspoon salt and 8 grinds pepper. Tie together the sprigs of oregano and rosemary with kitchen twine; add to the pot. Raise the heat to high and bring to a boil, using a potato masher to break up the tomatoes a bit.

2. Once the stew comes to a gentle boil, reduce the heat to medium low and cover, leaving the lid just slightly ajar. Simmer until the squash and lentils are tender, about 20 minutes. Uncover and stir in the chard leaves. Re-cover and cook until the chard is tender, about another 5 minutes. (If you end up with insufficient liquid, just add a bit more stock, and adjust the seasoning, if necessary.) Carefully remove and discard the herb bundle.

continued

1½ cups dried red lentils, sorted through and rinsed

¼ cup fresh-squeezed, strained lemon juice

8 sprigs fresh oregano

1 large sprig plus 1½ teaspoons minced fresh rosemary, divided

3 packed cups coarsely chopped Swiss chard leaves, stems removed and discarded, washed and spun dry

About 2 tablespoons unbleached all-purpose flour, for rolling out the puff pastry, divided

One 14-ounce package frozen puff pastry, such as Dufour®, thawed

1½ teaspoons minced fresh sage, divided

3. While the stew is cooking, line two baking sheets with sides with parchment paper to cover. Sprinkle about half of the flour on a large, clean surface. Unroll the puff pastry and sprinkle with some of the remaining flour. Roll out the pastry to a rectangle roughly 11 x 16 inches. With a sharp knife, cut out 4 rounds, each roughly 5½ x 6½ inches. Place 2 rounds on each lined baking sheet. Gather the dough scraps into a circle, sprinkle with a bit more flour, and roll out. Form a fifth round and place it on one of the baking sheets (make sure to leave at least 2 inches between the circles). Sprinkle the 5 dough rounds evenly with 1 teaspoon minced rosemary and 1 teaspoon minced sage. Cut a few slits in each of the circles (to prevent the pastry from puffing up too much). If the pastry is still cold, proceed to the next step. If not, place the baking sheets in the refrigerator and chill the dough.

4. Place the baking sheets with the cold pastry on two racks in the hot oven and bake until the dough circles are golden brown, puffed, and completely cooked through in the center, switching racks halfway through, 20 to 25 minutes total.

5. To serve, ladle about 2 cups of stew into large, shallow soup bowls. Top each portion with a puff pastry circle, and—if desired—garnish with some of the remaining ½ teaspoon minced rosemary and ½ teaspoon minced sage. Serve hot.

SERVING SUGGESTIONS: Since this dish is so filling, serve it with a light salad of radicchio and endive with pickled shallots and mushrooms. For dessert, opt for fresh pears with Stilton cheese and toasted walnuts, or baked apples stuffed with dried fruit and drizzled in maple syrup.

Grilled Portabella Mushroom Sandwiches with Basil-Lime Mayonnaise

SERVES 4

These sandwiches (make them vegan by using a vegan mayonnaise and substituting maple syrup for the honey) sing with the flavors of basil, lime, mustard, and honey. The creamy herby mayonnaise and sweet, crunchy carrots balance out the peppery watercress and sweet-and-sour grilled mushrooms. Try to pick mushroom caps that are flat; they're easier to marinate and will cook more quickly. Clean them well to remove any dirt.

¼ cup extra-virgin olive oil

¼ cup sherry or red-wine vinegar

1 large, juicy lime, zested and juiced, divided

2 tablespoons honey

1 tablespoon Dijon mustard

1 tablespoon brine from a jar of giardiniera (Italian pickled vegetables) or chopped green chiles

Scant 1¼ pounds portabella mushroom caps

¼ teaspoon coarse salt

½ cup mayonnaise

½ cup fresh basil leaves, packed

2 tablespoons vegetable oil

4 round rolls, split and toasted

1 cup shredded carrots

1 cup watercress or arugula leaves, washed and spun dry

1. In a large baking dish, whisk together the olive oil, vinegar, lime juice (you should have 3 tablespoons), honey, mustard, and brine. Add the mushroom caps and massage the marinade into both sides, coating them well. Let marinate at room temperature for at least 15 minutes and up to 1 hour. Remove the mushrooms from the marinade and sprinkle both sides evenly with the salt.

2. Meanwhile, combine the mayonnaise, basil, and lime zest (you should have about 1 teaspoon) in the bowl of a food processor. Purée until well combined, about 30 seconds (you should have ½ cup).

3. Brush a large nonstick grill pan with the vegetable oil, and heat over medium high (or heat the grill). When hot, add the mushrooms and cook until tender and charred (but not burned), turning over halfway through cooking, 7 to 9 minutes total.

4. Spread 2 tablespoons of the basil-lime mayo onto half of each roll. Top with a grilled mushroom, a quarter of the carrots, and a quarter of the watercress. Top with the other roll half, and serve immediately.

SERVING SUGGESTIONS: Round out the meal with paprika-dusted oven fries, and offer key lime pie for dessert.

Mexican Shepherd's Pie with Black Beans and Yams

SERVES 4 TO 6

This mild dish is perfect for all palates. For a heat-loving crowd, add some minced fresh jalapeños to the onion-pepper mixture or sprinkle with some cayenne pepper.

2 yams

1 cup grated Cheddar

½ cup 2% milk, at room temperature

4 tablespoons (½ stick) unsalted butter, melted

1⅛ teaspoons coarse salt, divided

10 grinds black pepper, divided

1 tablespoon canola oil

1 scant cup finely chopped red onions

¾ cup finely chopped red bell peppers

3 tablespoons finely chopped celery

1 teaspoon minced garlic

One 15-ounce can black beans, rinsed and drained

2 tablespoons tomato paste

1 tablespoon sherry or red-wine vinegar

1 teaspoon honey

¼ plus ⅛ teaspoon ground cumin, divided

¼ teaspoon ancho chili powder, divided

¾ to 1 cup sour cream, for serving

4 to 6 teaspoons chopped fresh cilantro leaves, for serving

1. Heat the oven to 400°F. Poke each yam all over with a knife, place in the microwave, and cook on high until very tender, about 13 minutes (this will depend on the strength of your microwave). When cool enough to handle, cut them open and scoop out the flesh; transfer 2½ cups to a medium-sized bowl (reserve any remainder for another use). Mash with a potato masher. While still hot, add the cheese, milk, butter, ¾ teaspoon salt, and 5 grinds pepper, and stir to mix well. Set aside.

2. Meanwhile, heat the oil in a 10-inch, heavy sauté pan (with high sides) over medium-high heat. When hot, add the onions, peppers, celery, and garlic, and sauté until the vegetables are softened, about 6 minutes. Add the beans, tomato paste, vinegar, honey, ¼ plus ⅛ teaspoon salt, ¼ teaspoon cumin, ⅛ teaspoon chili powder, and 5 grinds pepper. Cook, stirring to combine the ingredients well, for another 5 minutes. Set aside off the heat.

3. Grease a 2-quart rectangular glass baking dish with nonstick cooking spray. Add the bean mixture and spread evenly. Top with the yam mixture and spread evenly. Sprinkle with the remaining ⅛ teaspoon chili powder and ⅛ teaspoon cumin. Bake until hot and the edges of the yam mixture turn golden brown, about 35 minutes. Serve with sour cream and cilantro.

SERVING SUGGESTIONS: Ideal for cozy family suppers, this leftover-friendly, quick-to-prepare entrée would be delicious served with a jìcama-orange-radish salad with lime vinaigrette. Mexican hot chocolate or lime sorbet with pomegranate seeds would be ideal for dessert.

Stuffing with Apples, Dried Cherries, and Herb Brown Butter

SERVES 6

Why limit this tender, flavorful dish to Thanksgiving? Serve it year-round as an entrée. Thanks to vegetarian grain meat sausage, the dish has a meaty quality sure to satisfy vegetarians and carnivores alike.

4 cups ½-inch cubes cornbread

4 cups ½-inch cubes sourdough bread

6 tablespoons (½ stick plus 2 tablespoons) unsalted butter, divided

Scant 2 cups ¼-inch-thick half-moons celery

Scant 1½ cups thinly sliced leeks

½ cup finely chopped red onions

2½ teaspoons minced garlic

3 cups ½-inch cubes peeled and cored Granny Smith apples

4 ready-to-eat smoked apple vegetarian sausage, such as Field Roast®, casings removed and discarded and insides crumbled

3 tablespoons minced fresh sage leaves

1 tablespoon minced fresh rosemary

1. Heat the oven to 375°F. Pour the cornbread and sourdough cubes onto a baking sheet with sides. Once the oven is hot, toast until golden brown and dried out, about 20 minutes. Remove from the oven and set aside (leave the oven on).

2. Meanwhile, heat 2 tablespoons butter in a 12-inch, heavy, nonstick sauté pan (with 2- to 3-inch-high sides) over medium-high heat. Once the butter is melted, add the celery, leeks, red onions, and garlic, and sauté until softened, about 8 minutes. Add the apples and crumbled sausage and simmer, stirring occasionally and breaking up the sausage with a wooden spoon, until the apples are tender, about 6 minutes. Remove from the heat.

3. Meanwhile, melt the remaining 4 tablespoons butter over medium heat in a small, heavy frying pan. Once the butter is melted, let it bubble for a minute, and then stir in the fresh sage and rosemary leaves. Let bubble for 1 minute, until the butter turns very light golden, and then remove from the heat and set aside. Meanwhile, place the cranberries in a small bowl, cover with very hot water, and let sit to soften, 10 to 15 minutes. Drain.

4. In a large bowl, combine the cranberries, bread cubes, vegetable-apple-sausage mixture, herb butter (scrape it out of the pan), vegetable broth, parsley, beaten eggs, salt, and pepper, using tongs to mix gently but well. Spray the entire inside of a 9 x 13 x 2-inch glass baking dish with cooking spray. Pour the stuffing mixture inside and spread evenly, flattening it down.

½ cup sweetened dried
   cranberries

2 cups reduced-sodium
   vegetable broth

⅓ cup finely chopped fresh
   flat-leaf parsley leaves

2 large eggs, beaten well

1 teaspoon coarse salt

8 grinds black pepper

5. Cover with aluminum foil and bake for 40 minutes. Uncover and cook for another 20 minutes, until golden brown on top and tender and fluffy inside. Serve.

SERVING SUGGESTIONS: Pair with braised winter greens. For dessert, serve pumpkin pie or a cranberry tart.

TRY THIS: If you prefer your stuffing more savory than sweet, use all sourdough and no cornbread. Substitute sautéed mushrooms and an Italian-flavored grain sausage for the dried cranberries.

Pumpkin Lasagna with Brown Butter and Sage

SERVES 8 TO 10

This fall dish is halfway between a traditional lasagna and a noodle kugel, a sweet Jewish noodle dish of farmer or cottage cheese and egg noodles. The tender noodles surround the sweet pumpkin mixture; creamy cheese adds richness and saltiness.

1¾ teaspoons coarse salt, plus extra for the pasta water, divided

5 tablespoons olive oil, divided

1 pound fresh lasagna sheets

Two 15-ounce cans pure pumpkin (not pie filling)

4 tablespoons (½ stick) unsalted butter

1 heaping, packed tablespoon finely chopped fresh sage leaves

2 tablespoons maple syrup

½ teaspoon freshly grated nutmeg

13 grinds black pepper, divided

⅛ teaspoon crushed red pepper flakes

One 32-ounce container ricotta (full fat or part skim)

1¼ cups freshly grated Parmigiano-Reggiano, divided

2 large eggs, beaten

1 teaspoon lemon zest

1. Heat the oven to 375°F. Fill a large pot two-thirds full of heavily salted water, cover, and bring to a boil over high heat. Pour 3 tablespoons oil onto a baking sheet with sides, and place a colander in the sink. Once the water is boiling, add the pasta, stir for a minute to separate the sheets, and continue boiling until al dente, about another 2 or 3 minutes (follow the package instructions). Pour the cooked pasta into the colander in the sink to drain, and then onto the baking sheet. Use tongs and a hand mitt to carefully peel apart the pasta sheets, greasing them with the oil so they don't stick to each other.

2. Meanwhile, pour the pumpkin into a medium-sized bowl. Heat the butter in a 10-inch, heavy, nonstick sauté pan over medium heat. Once it melts, let it continue cooking until it begins to smell nutty and turn a light golden brown, 3 or 4 minutes. Add the sage and continue cooking, stirring occasionally, for 2 minutes. Pour the sage brown butter into the bowl with the pumpkin, then stir in the maple syrup, 1 teaspoon salt, the nutmeg, 5 grinds pepper, and the red pepper flakes.

3. In another medium-sized bowl, stir together the ricotta, 1 cup Parmigiano-Reggiano, the beaten eggs, lemon zest, ¾ teaspoon salt, and 8 grinds pepper, combining them well.

continued

4. Pour the remaining 2 tablespoons oil into a 9 x 13 x 2-inch glass baking dish and brush over the entire interior surface to grease. Place two lasagna sheets over the bottom to cover. Pour in half of the pumpkin mixture and spread evenly. Top with two more lasagna sheets and then 1½ cups of the ricotta mixture. Top with two more lasagna sheets and the remainder of the pumpkin mixture, spreading evenly. Top with two more lasagna sheets and another 1½ cups of the ricotta mixture. Top with two more sheets of lasagna, and the remaining 1 cup of the ricotta mixture. Sprinkle evenly with the remaining ¼ cup Parmigiano-Reggiano.

5. Place the lasagna in the oven and bake until the ricotta mixture puffs up and turns golden brown on the sides and all of the Parmigiano-Reggiano on top has melted, about 45 minutes. Let sit for at least 15 minutes at room temperature, and then serve.

SERVING SUGGESTION: Serve this rich entrée with an arugula salad, with pomegranate sorbet and orange segments for dessert.

TRY THIS: Vary the recipe by substituting other layers for the pumpkin. Sautéed spinach and mushrooms or oven-roasted tomatoes would be delicious.

Risotto with Pumpkin, Mushrooms, and Fontina

SERVES 4

This super-cheesy, pumpkin-hued risotto is rich and creamy. Best prepared right before serving, the risotto can be reheated with additional broth to thin it out.

1 to 2 tablespoons dried wild mushrooms, such as porcini

8 cups reduced-sodium vegetable broth

5 tablespoons (½ stick plus 1 tablespoon) unsalted butter, divided

1½ teaspoons minced garlic

9 ounces white button mushrooms, stems discarded and caps sliced

1 cup small-dice peeled butternut squash

1½ teaspoons coarse salt, divided

15 grinds black pepper, divided

1 cup finely chopped red onions

1¾ cups risotto rice, such as arborio

1 cup fruity white wine, such as Viognier

One 15-ounce can unsweetened pumpkin or butternut squash

About ⅔ pound Fontina, rind removed, grated

continued

1. Place the dried wild mushrooms on a medium-sized piece of cheesecloth. Shape into a bundle and close with kitchen twine. Add the mushroom sack plus the broth to a medium-sized heavy saucepan, and bring to a simmer over high heat. Once the broth is simmering, reduce the heat to medium low to low to keep warm.

2. Add 2 tablespoons butter to a 10-inch, heavy sauté pan and heat over medium high. Once the butter melts, add the garlic and sauté until aromatic, no more than 1 minute. Add the white mushrooms and sauté until golden brown and tender and the liquid has evaporated, stirring occasionally, about 6 minutes. Add the squash and continue to sauté, stirring well, until tender, about another 6 minutes. Stir in ¼ teaspoon salt and 5 grinds pepper, and set aside off the heat.

3. Meanwhile, melt the remaining 3 tablespoons butter in a large heavy Dutch oven over medium-high heat. Once the butter has melted, add the onions and sauté until soft and aromatic, about 3 minutes. Add the rice and sauté for 1 minute. Off the heat, add the wine. Return the pot to the heat, stir in the pumpkin, and bring to a boil. Once the mixture reaches a boil, reduce the heat to medium.

4. Add the simmering broth in ½-cup ladlefuls to the rice-onion mixture, and stir with a wooden spoon. Wait until most of the liquid evaporates (about 2 minutes), and then add another ladleful of simmering broth to the rice-onion mixture. Repeat about ten more times (being careful not to add the mushroom

continued

½ cup freshly grated Parmigiano-Reggiano

1 tablespoon minced fresh sage leaves, plus 1 tablespoon fresh sage leaves cut into chiffonade, for garnish (optional)

1 tablespoon maple syrup

¼ teaspoon freshly grated nutmeg

sack to the rice mixture) until you use most of the broth and the rice is tender but not mushy; the entire process will take about 22 minutes. Turn off the heat.

5. Stir in the cooked mushroom-squash mixture, the two cheeses, the minced sage, syrup, nutmeg, and remaining 1¼ teaspoons salt and 10 grinds pepper. Continue stirring until the cheese melts. Serve immediately, garnishing—if desired—with additional sage.

SERVING SUGGESTIONS: Pair with a radicchio and green apple salad, the wine you used to make the dish, and hazelnut cookies for dessert.

TRY THIS: Relatively large and hard, butternut squash can seem intimidating to prep, but the process is quick and easy—all you need is a sharp chef's knife or cleaver. First, lay the squash on a cutting board. Cut it in half crosswise, so you're left with one rectangular piece and one bulb-shaped piece (this makes working with the squash more manageable). One at a time, stand each piece on the cutting board. Carefully, use your knife to cut all around the sides to remove the hard skin. Slice each peeled piece in half lengthwise. Use a spoon to scoop out the seeds (if you like, you can roast them after removing the stringy flesh). Now, dice the flesh.

Vegetarian Resources

Visit these websites for more information about eating a vegetarian diet.

Compassion Over Killing, www.cok.net

Farm Animal Rights Movement, www.farmusa.org

Meatless Monday, www.meatlessmonday.com

North American Vegetarian Society, www.navs-online.org

The Savvy Vegetarian, www.savvyvegetarian.com

The Vegetarian Resource Group and Vegetarian Journal, www.vrg.org

The Vegetarian Society, www.vegsoc.org

Vegetarian Times Magazine, www.vegetariantimes.com

VegNews Magazine, www.vegnews.com

VegSource, www.vegsource.com

VegVine, www.vegvine.com

Metric Equivalents

Liquid/Dry Measures

U.S.	METRIC
¼ teaspoon	1.25 milliliters
½ teaspoon	2.5 milliliters
1 teaspoon	5 milliliters
1 tablespoon (3 teaspoons)	15 milliliters
1 fluid ounce (2 tablespoons)	30 milliliters
¼ cup	60 milliliters
⅓ cup	80 milliliters
½ cup	120 milliliters
1 cup	240 milliliters
1 pint (2 cups)	480 milliliters
1 quart (4 cups; 32 ounces)	960 milliliters
1 gallon (4 quarts)	3.84 liters
1 ounce (by weight)	28 grams
1 pound	454 grams
2.2 pounds	1 kilogram

Oven Temperatures

°F	GAS MARK	°C
250	½	120
275	1	140
300	2	150
325	3	165
350	4	180
375	5	190
400	6	200
425	7	220
450	8	230
475	9	240
500	10	260
550	Broil	290

Index

If you like this book, you'll love *Fine Cooking*.